Mary Wentworth Newman

The Golden Dawn

And Other Stories

Mary Wentworth Newman

The Golden Dawn
And Other Stories

ISBN/EAN: 9783337004774

Printed in Europe, USA, Canada, Australia, Japan

Cover: Foto ©Thomas Meinert / pixelio.de

More available books at **www.hansebooks.com**

FRONTISPIECE.   [See Preface.

THE GOLDEN GATE

SERIES.

GOLDEN DAWN.

SAN·FRANCISCO.
A. ROMAN & C? PUBLISHERS,

John Andrew · Bos

THE

GOLDEN DAWN

AND

OTHER STORIES.

BY MAY WENTWORTH.

Oh rivers that flow o'er the shining sand,
Through wonderous mazes in golden land ;
Flamingoes that flit through the orange bowers,
With plumage as bright as the tropical flowers ;
Rich lights of the North, that with roseate glow
Illumine the pure white mantle of snow ;
And wild waves that dance o'er the billowy sea,
Bring mystical tales of beauty to me.

NEW YORK:
A. ROMAN & COMPANY, PUBLISHERS.
SAN FRANCISCO :
417 & 419 MONTGOMERY STREET.
1870.

DEDICATION.

PREFACE.

SITTING in my quiet study, and looking dreamily out from my thought-window, I see around me little graceful forms, with dancing feet and dimpled hands.

There are beautiful beaming eyes, luminous with eager gladness, cheeks like the Spring rosebuds, and cherry lips that coax so winsomely for fairy tales.

Again with curious warp and woof I weave the mystic story, and watch the varying light and shade that flit across these childish faces.

How eagerly they listen, and every impression sets its signet on their unformed hearts.

It is a joy to fill these April days with

brightness, yet for the little ones I crave a greater happiness.

Mid all the freshness of the morning, that casts its radiance on them and makes the world enchanting, and all the pleasant home endearments, I would have them sometimes stop and think upon the coming, the silent coming of the Golden Dawn.

MAY WENTWORTH.

San-Francisco, 1869.

TABLE OF CONTENTS.

FAIRY TALES.

THE GOLDEN DAWN.

On a moss-covered rock down by the sea played a beautiful child. With rosy fingers she gathered the sea-weed, delighting in its delicate tracery and varied tints.

All around her danced the emerald waves, in their pretty white caps, laving the foot of the gray rock and talking their pleasant summer day talk. It was now low tide, and quite safe for the little one to play on the old rock that had stood for ages unmoved by the changeful temper of the restless deep.

Her sunny curls strayed in pretty disorder over her dimpled shoulders and her

little straw hat, filled with shells and flowers, hung upon her dainty arm.

" The sea-weed is prettier than the china-
aster in mother's garden," thought the child.
" I wonder the mermaids can spare it; but
old Nurse Minta says they have such beautiful things down under the sun-lit sea.

" Great chambers of wonderful gems,
emeralds as green as the waves, sapphires as
blue as the sky, and radiant opals, far richer
than all the jewels in mother's pearl casket,
that she just allows me to look at when I
am good, but will never let me take in my
hand."

At this moment the beaming eyes of the
happy child fell upon a strange looking shell
that lay at her feet. It was of a soft rosy
hue and shaped like a trumpet. With eager
hands she grasped it, exclaiming: "It is
the mermaid's whistle ; now I can call them
to come and play with me."

Placing the shell to her crimson lips she blew a clear musical note, that the little dancing waves caught up and carried far out to sea. Then with a sweet lisping voice she sung :

> Oh ! mermaid, come out of the sea,
> Come out of the sea and play with me ;
> Bring me an opal, clear and bright,
> Bring me a diamond of luminous white,
> Bring me a branch of the coral tree,
> On this old gray rock I would play with thee.

Again she sounded a longer note from the mermaid's trumpet, and sure enough she saw floating upon the sea a great mass of silken tresses, and in a moment the entrancing face of the mermaid was raised above the waves.

"I can not come out of the water, little girl," she said, " the sun would burn me ; but you can come in to me, it is cool and delicious here. I can not walk as you do, and really it must be very uncomfortable on the dry rocks and sanded shore."

"I am afraid of the waves," replied the child, "they leap about so, I should lose my breath; but if you please we will go home to mother. In the garden there is a plum tree, and all the branches are red with ripe fruit, and because you will be company, mother will give you some."

"But I can not live on the shore," said the mermaid, "if you should only visit the palaces of the deep you would laugh at 'mother's garden,' a pleasant homely old place, no doubt, but not like the gardens of the sea. There are such glorious coral trees, some that wave their rosy branches like great fans, and others white and shining spread over many miles, and rise up to the surface of the waters. Then it is only the waste sea-weed that you have here, but down in the sea it is really beautiful and bright in coloring as the tints of the rainbow, and the flowers are like the stars of night.

" The palace of the king is more wonderful than a dream. Tall columns of jasper support the stately dome, which is studded with great carbuncles, and all through the fretwork of the windows gleam rich luminous stones, diamonds, pearls and opals. The courts are paved with many-hued marbles, and the fountains play in soft delicious melody.

" At night, when the moon shines through the waters, it is as though a flood of beaming silver floated over all, but when the morning comes on, all the gold of the sunshine sinks down under the waves. Then it is glorious! it is royal! Nothing in all the world of waters is like the silent coming of the golden dawn."

The child was bewildered and delighted with the gorgeous description of the mermaid. She wished to visit the stately palaces, and roam through the pleasant gardens of the sea, but above all she longed to hail the coming of the golden dawn. "I should like to go with you, pretty mermaid," she said, "only for my mother. I love dear mother so, and then the old garden is pleasant; all my life I have played in it, and now the red plums are ripening in the sunshine."

"Silly child," said the mermaid, holding out her white arms to clasp the little one, "can you forget the glory of the golden dawn."

The child, fascinated and bewildered, was almost ready to spring forward into the tempting waters. Still she hesitated and then drew back exclaiming, "No! no, I can not, I can not leave mother."

Just then there was a great rushing sound that seemed to break the witching spell that had bound her with its mystic power. The tide was coming in, and all around the old gray rock dashed the angry breakers with sullen roar.

The mermaid sank slowly out of sight under the darkened waves, and in the midst of the waters the little child was left alone. The night was coming on, and the sky was black with clouds. She looked fearfully around, but it was no use! the way to the shore was all cut off by the breakers which had rushed in, and surrounded her in a moment of time. " Oh, mother," she cried, " I shall never, never see you again, the hungry waves will devour me. Even the mermaid has gone, and I dare not go alone to the sea-king's palace. I shall die on this desolate rock, and the golden dawn will never come to me ; but oh, mother, how can I leave you, mother ?"

Into the darkness of the storm-clad night sobbed the little child and around her dashed the furious breakers, rising every moment higher and higher, till at last nothing was left only the summit of the rock to which the little trembling hands clung piteously.

Hour after hour passed on, and still the storm raged furiously. The warm life of the child was chilled, and her dainty robes, wet and heavy, clung closely about her quivering form.

Now every moment she was growing fainter, but somehow the bitterness of her anguish had passed away.

In a low voice she murmured, " Oh, mother, it will come, and now I am waiting, only waiting for the coming of the golden dawn.

" It is not on earth nor in the shining chambers of the sea, but in Heaven, mother, where God is. I do not want to leave you, mother, but think, oh, think of the radiant glory of the golden dawn."

The storm died away and the ebbing tide bore back to the sea the waves that all night long had lashed the rock with hungry tongues. The morning came and with it an anxious crowd of watchers gathered upon the white sanded shore.

The mother was there, and it was her loving eye that first caught a glimpse of the little white robes that enfolded the form of her darling. With an agonizing wail she cried, " Oh, my child! my child! "

It was the beloved voice, and for a moment the sound called back the feeling life that was going out with the tide.

The child softly clasped her hands. " It is mother," she whispered, " but the golden dawn is coming; I am going out to meet it, mother, dear mother."

All the crowd rushed forward together, but in her loving arms the mother clasped only the lifeless form of her darling; the pure spirit had entered forever upon the glory of the golden dawn.

2

BLANCHE AND OLIVIA.

In a pleasant hacienda in the Southern Californian land, lived an old Spanish woman who was greatly beloved by all her neighbors, for her kindness of heart.

None were so poor and wretched, that the widow could not take their hand, and none so guilty that she would not seek an excuse for their errors. "God only knows how they were tempted," she would say, "Of his great mercy he can forgive even the chief of sinners." Her whole time was devoted to the duties of religion, deeds of charity and the care of her two daughters, who were beautiful young maidens just budding into womanhood. The eldest was called Blanche, on account of the purity and fairness of her complexion, which in that warm climate was a marvel of beauty.

The youngest, named Olivia, was like the lovely daughters of the orient, rich and warm in complexion, with large lustrous dark eyes changing with every varied mood; at times full of dreamy softness, but often flashing with the fire of uncontrolled passion. Blanche was gentle in disposition, ready to yield and full of tenderness. At the least harshness her soft blue eyes would sparkle with the glistening dew of tears.

The good mother spent many hours in prayer for her youngest child. She was never weary of teaching her to be mild and good. Still Olivia was passionate and selfish, yet her affectionate disposition and agreeable vivacity made her a favorite with the young maidens, and her great beauty was the admiration of all the gallant hidalgos for miles around. In fact, there was nobody so delightful as Olivia, when every thing pleased her.

One day as the young girls sat upon the piazza at their embroidery, they saw a most curious looking little creature coming through the gate, and up the pathway to the house. She was dressed in a crimson farthingale, with the ever-present Spanish shawl over her head. At first they thought it was a poor lame child about eight years old, she leaned so heavily upon her staff and hobbled along making a great ado, but when she came nearer and threw back the shawl they saw the face of an old woman, ugly and yellow as saffron.

Olivia could not resist the impulse to laugh at the funny looking little creature, so grotesque in her dress and manners, but Blanche ran in and brought out a low easy chair for her to sit on. She sank into the comfortable seat as though she was very weary.

"It is gala time with you now, my pretty
Señoritas," she said, in a grumbling tone,
"but the golden mist of the morning will soon
pass, then see how you will like the burden
and heat of the noon day, or the cold twilight of the evening."

Olivia only laughed at this, but Blanche
whispered softly "I see nothing to laugh at sister, do not grieve the poor creature I beg you."
Then aloud she said in a pleasant tone, "You
are weary Goodie, and must be hungry and
thirsty, shall I bring you something to eat?"

"Yes! yes!" answered the old woman
impatiently, "go children, both of you, bring
me something delicate and nice, I am too
old for coarse food; that will do for the young
who have always good appetites."

Blanche ran quickly and soon returned
with snow white bread, light and flakey,
fresh eggs, honey in the comb, and a bowl of
rich thick cream.

"This will do with fruit," said the old woman.

It was yet early in the season, and the fruit was ripe on only two trees in the garden, one of these a delicate plum tree belonged to Blanche, and the other a fine apricot was always called Olivia's tree; the girls had decided to give a little treat to their friends, and no one had been allowed to touch the fruit, there was so little ripe, and the young people were coming that evening. Blanche ran quickly into the garden. There glistening in the morning sunshine among the bright-green leaves, hung the tempting plums. Yet there were so very few that Blanche sighed as she looked at them.

" I will eat none myself," she said ; " it will be pleasure enough to see the others enjoy it, and I am not sorry to give this poor old woman my share."

So she began picking the precious fruit,

and the flecks of golden sunshine, shining through the branches of the trees, danced in the mazes of her beautiful hair, and stealing through her liquid eyes, rested in her heart. She gathered some grape leaves wet with dew, and placing them in a pretty glass dish arranged the ripe plums upon them, and carried them in to the old woman with a pleasant smile.

All this time Olivia sat at her embroidery humming a lively Spanish air.

She thought of her apricot tree and the pleasant sunshine glinting the delicious ripe fruit; there was far more of it than on the plum tree, for it grew in the most sheltered spot of the whole garden.

"The greedy old woman" she thought, "does she suppose I shall give her the first early fruit of my tree, when there is hardly enough for myself and my friends? That will do for the silly Blanche, who never thinks enough of her young friends, or she could not give every thing to an old hag like this, who is ugly as a witch."

Yet, with all her sophistry she did not feel quite comfortable.

When the old woman had eaten, she said to Blanche, " You are a good child, I have enjoyed your fruit very much, and now I shall reward you."

Putting her hand into the pocket of her farthingale she drew out a beautiful little enameled box that opened with a secret spring. Both the girls drew near her, and touching the spring she disclosed to their admiring gaze, two rings of curious workmanship, and great value. One was a pearl cluster, and in the center was a large liquid gem as clear as a dew-drop. The other was a rich garnet that flashed in the sunshine like a live coal.

"How beautiful!" exclaimed Olivia,

flushed with the excitement of pleasant surprise.

"Yes, very beautiful," answered the little woman, "and so is the fresh bloom upon your apricots in the garden."

Olivia hung down her head with shame, and pouted out her pretty lips in vexation, wishing very much she had been less selfish.

Blanche was so sorry for her sister's mortification, that she laid her little white hand upon the old woman's arm, saying, in a pleading voice, "Goodie, please excuse Olivia this time, and give her the ring you intended for me."

"No, dear child," replied the old woman, "you shall have this rare pearl which is pure as your own white heart. For your sake I will give your sister the garnet which is like her fiery nature."

"Listen my children!" she continued. "These rings are the talismans of your lives.

So long, my Blanche, as you keep your heart pure and truthful, the pearl will be clear and beautiful, and your life will be prosperous and happy. But guard well your ways, my dear child ; and you, Olivia, subdue the selfishness of your disposition, or like the red fire of the garnet your passions will burn your life out.

"Preserve these rings with the greatest care, for they will control your future destiny, and be a guide to your life and actions. Above all, Olivia, beware of the fiery light of the garnet; you are only safe when its red light softens to a clear rosy glow."

Then the old woman walked slowly away ; but when Blanche saw how feeble she seemed, she ran after her and offered her arm, saying, "good mother, lean upon me, I would like to help you on your way ;" and they went on together talking pleasantly until they came to a great wood.

When they had passed into the shadow of

the giant trees the old woman bade Blanche
"good-bye," saying, "go home now, my child,
to your kind mother; strive always to keep
your heart spotless like the beautiful pearl.
So may God bless you."

Then she disappeared among the thick
trees of the wood and Blanche hastened home-
ward for the twilight was coming on. She
was a timid maiden and the great rocks and
trees startled her at every step. They looked
so like huge giants waving their long arms
at her. When at last she reached home she
was quite pale with fright and fatigue.

She found the dear mother had been very
anxious about her. She threw her arms
around her neck, saying, "mother, forgive the
uneasiness I have caused you, but the woman was so old and infirm and the way so
long I could not return sooner."

The mother kissed her and smoothed her
silken hair, saying, " hasten now, my daugh-

ter, the young people have come." From the receiving room she heard the sounds of mirth and happiness. Olivia and the young friends were enjoying the ripe fruit, but by the time Blanche was ready to go into the room it was all eaten, and they were just starting home for it was quite late.

They greeted the young girl with smiles. "They had missed her; indeed she must not run away again," they said. Then with pleasant adieus they went away.

Blanche helped the mother to wash the dishes and put the house in order, but Olivia sat down in the corner looking at her beautiful ring and dreaming of the future. By and by she said, "Blanche, there is to be a great ball at Don Juan Realto's. We are invited and must go."

"I should like it very much if mother is willing," replied Blanche.

The mother gave her ready consent, and

they sat round the pleasant fire together, the young girls talking of the coming festival and their young friends, who would be present, and the mother living over again the days of her youth in the enjoyment of her children.

The intervening days before the ball were very busy ones for the young girls, who with the mother's help made their simple white dresses. When the evening came, and the last ribbon was adjusted, and the wreaths of natural flowers twined about their abundant tresses,-though the mother reproached herself for her pride, she could not help thinking, that in all the country it would be impossible to find two such beautiful girls as her own.

Just before they started Olivia touched the fair cheek of her sister with her cherry lips, saying, " How pretty you look to-night, you do not need your ring. It will look beautifully beside my garnet. Let me wear it just for to-night."

"Sister," replied Blanche, "do not ask me! remember what the old woman said. I shall not feel quite comfortable without it."

"Oh, if you do not wish to oblige your sister, never mind, but I think I could take as good care of it as you could." Olivia's bright face was darkened with a frown, and her sparkling eyes flashed with anger.

"Take it, Olivia" said Blanche, with a touch of sadness in her voice. She drew the ring from her finger and gave it to her sister, saying, " please be careful of it, dear."

"Do not be silly, my darling little sister," replied Olivia; her face now radiant with smiles.

" How pretty it looks beside the garnet," she added; " much better than on your hand, indeed one would hardly notice it alone ; but come now let us go."

As they kissed the mother and went out, the good woman sighed heavily for Olivia's selfishness.

" Will the child never overcome her self-love " she said, sadly.

Above all things she longed to see her children gentle and good, and for this she earnestly prayed.

There were not two more charming maidens at the ball than the sisters. So different in every respect yet equally beautiful.

The young Don Alberto Realto admired them both so greatly that he could hardly decide which possessed the charm that could brighten his life, and strange to say both the young girls thought him the handsomest young hidalgo in the whole country.

It was a pleasant evening for all, and the sisters danced in every set until the ball was over, and that was delightful though they were quite weary. They went home talking of all the gay young señoritas and hidalgos, but most of all of Don Alberto.

"How brilliant he is," said Olivia, "yet how his proud eye softened while he talked to me; sister, he has a heart as brave as a lion, yet as soft as a woman's."

"Yes! he was so gentle and patient in listening to the old Señora Bianca's long stories, when I knew he wanted to be dancing with the young señoritas."

"Poh!" said Olivia, "that was silly of him, but for all that he is delightful."

Thus the two sisters talked on till they reached home. It was late, and they went directly to their own chamber. When they were undressed Blanche said, "now Olivia give me back my ring; I shall sleep better with it on my finger."

Olivia raised her hand to take it off but to her great surprise both rings were gone.

"Both gone!" she exclaimed, "how could

I have lost them! " and in her passionate way she burst into an uncontrollable fit of weeping.

Blanche turned pale as death.

"The talisman of our lives gone!" she cried; a shudder of superstition chilling her heart.

They commenced looking carefully for the lost treasure. But nowhere in the folds of Olivia's dress, on the carpet of their chamber, nor in the passage ways could the rings be found.

It was no use searching in the darkness, so they went to bed, and Olivia soon wept herself to sleep, but Blanche lay till the dawning, sleepless and trembling with fevered imaginings.

In the gray twilight she rose softly and went to the mother's room; there she told all her fears and troubles, and nestling her head in the loving bosom that had soothed her infancy, was comforted.

The mother was sorry for the loss of the

pretty jewels but she laughed at the fears of her children.

"It is only a superstitious dread awakened by the curious myth the old woman was pleased to tell you, my dears," said she, kindly. "She knew what silly girls you were and amused herself with you."

Again they searched for the treasures every where there could be a hope of finding them. They even sent to Don Juan Realto's, yet nothing but disappointment came of it.

Weeks passed by and the rings were almost forgotten. Don Alberto was often at the hacienda; he was still the favorite of both sisters though Blanche avoided him. At last he caught a glimpse of the passionate shadow that haunted Olivia.

"She is beautiful as a dream," he thought, "but the storm clouds frighten me; only Blanche, dear, true, unselfish Blanche shall be the angel of my house."

Thus the young hidalgo decided, and after that he sought only Blanche every where.

Then the shadow darkened. Olivia grew more proud and selfish ; and in her closet the mother wept and prayed more than ever.

One day a stranger rode up to the house ; he had known the father years ago, and came to see the mother and daughters.

He was hospitably received, and the widow sat upon the piazza and talked with him in a low sad tone, and in her eyes the tears glistened in memory of the happier days.

He was a strange dark man, with fierce fiery eyes, and what seemed very odd with his complexion, his beard was quite red.

"Was there ever such a monster," whispered Olivia, "yet in his house which is like an old castle, there is one room filled with great bags of gold."

Blanche looked at the coarse cruel face and shrank away.

"Let us go into the garden while he talks with the dear mother; she will say some good thing which may make his heart better."

"He is like a prince," said Olivia. "It is glorious to be so very rich that one can never count his money."

Just then the stranger turned his head and his eyes met Olivia's. His lips parted with a smile and from out the thick red beard shone his teeth white and glittering.

The young girls turned to run into the garden but he called them.

"Come here, my pretty señoritas," he said, in a voice of silvery sweetness.

As they approached him Olivia shuddered. Her eye fell upon his hand, white as a woman's but strong and beautifully formed. There upon his taper finger, flashing out in the sunshine, she saw the fiery garnet, her ring, the talisman of her life.

"Oh, Blanche!" she cried, thrilled with ter-

ror, " he has my ring upon his finger, my
lost ring! "

Blanche looked eagerly. There was the
ring! She knew it well. In all the world
there was not another so full of blinding fire.

Trembling with eagerness Olivia approached the stranger.

"The ring," she said timidly, "where did
you find that ring?"

He held it up to the light till in its bril-
liancy it seemed to absorb all the sunshine,
and change it into a fierce red glare.

The stranger smiled again, and the white
teeth glittered fearfully.

"This ring," he said, in his softest tones,
" has a history, and one day," he added, turning to Olivia, "I shall place it upon your
finger, and you will know all."

Olivia would have fainted but her great
pride sustained her, and Blanche, who saw
how pale she was, handed her a glass of

water; then they went out, and the mother noticing their strange emotion followed them.

Again she laughed at their fears.

" My poor silly children, the old woman has bewitched you. Every like is not the same. Let me hear no more of this nonsense. Now go, my darlings, and compose your-selves, then come and help me to entertain the dear father's friend."

From that day the strange gentleman be-came a frequent visitor at the widow's house, and in a short time proposed for the hand of the fair Olivia.

She could not entirely overcome the repug-nance she had at first felt for him.

He was old enough to be her father, but he was immensely rich, and this to Olivia's luxurious, selfish nature and pride, seemed the only key that could open the strongly bar-red gate of happiness. There was something very repulsive in the red beard that covered

his swarthy face, and the red brows that
frowned over his fierce black eyes. "But
one can not have every thing," she thought;
"I will be a princess and live in a stately
palace."

Thus she became the rich hidalgo's bride,
and again the fiery garnet flashed upon her
finger. It was the pledge of their betrothal.

There was a princely wedding, and
Blanche was the bridesmaid.

She looked like a pure lily in her white
fleecy robes, and Olivia like a gorgeous tulip.

After the ceremony, Don Alberto was so
fortunate as to find Blanche where he could
whisper his charming secret to her.

He loved her so dearly she could make
life so sunny for him; and he talked on as
lovers will, till at last taking her soft white
hand in his, he pressed upon her finger the
betrothal ring ; clear beautiful pearls set in a
plain circlet of gold

A flush of excitement deepened the soft blush of pleasure that glowed upon the young girl's cheek.

"My ring!" she exclaimed joyously, and placing her hand in Alberto's, she added, "found at last!"

Then Alberto told her how he had bought it of a curious old woman who had told him it would bring him a life's happiness.

They laughed and talked pleasantly till Blanche thought of the fiery garnet, then, with a paler cheek and a heavy sigh, she told Alberto the strange story.

With the magic of love the young hidalgo soothed her fears, and they were very happy.

There was a pallor upon Olivia's cheek when she was told of the new betrothal, and a tremor of the voice, but she would not have given up her pride of wealth and state, no, not even for the dear love of Don Alberto.

On the morrow Olivia went to the rich hacienda of her husband. In the stately castle there were great rejoicings. Olivia was now the Grand Señora, and upon her lily white hand flashed the red garnet which absorbed into its magic fire all the warm, glorious sunshine, which should have shone upon her, and made her heart warm and happy.

In a few months Blanche was married. Don Alberto was not immensely rich, but with his strong manhood and energy their home was always one of plenty, and the sunshine that Blanche scattered everywhere around her made it the home of happiness.

Years passed by, and at long intervals the sisters exchanged visits; but between them somehow the pleasant confidence of childhood had passed away.

Blanche wept over this after every visit.
The splendor of her sister's home op-
pressed her. Though Olivia's cheek grew
pale and wan, her proud, passionate nature was unchanged, and upon her finger
shone the garnet more red and fiery than
ever.

At last, to the lordly castle came a son
and heir, and the hidalgo, who had long
been estranged from his wife, in the impulse
of this new affection, bent over and pressed
a kiss upon her forehead.

"Olivia!" he said, softly.

She opened her beautiful, dark eyes, and
though a shudder passed through her heart
at the sight of the repulsive face, she raised
her white hand and taking the red beard
she pressed it to her bloodless lips.   Then
the dark fire of the garnet grew paler ; a
strong, proud passion had been crushed out.

To the peaceful home of Blanche came the

swift messenger,—" The Grand Señora was dying !"

Blanche and Alberto started and traveled with the greatest speed, but when they arrived the shadow of the dread king had crossed the threshold before them. Already his cold breath had swept over the beautiful face, and there remained only one moment of time.

Blanche bent over the sister, weeping and crying, " Olivia! Olivia! speak to me but one word, beloved! but one word!"

Again the beautiful eyes opened, and Olivia whispered " Oh! my sister, there was nothing left of it all! nothing but ashes! ashes! My child would have saved me!" Then the eyes closed, and the shadow deepened, still, with a faint voice she whispered, " Our Father, who art in heaven, forgive us our sins for Christ's sake."

Over the river had passed the troubled

spirit into the unknown land of the dim hereafter.

Blanche stood by the bed-side weeping and calling, "My sister! Olivia, my sister!" She took the cold hand in hers and pressed it to her lips. On the taper finger was the talismanic ring, but all the fire,—the red glowing light of the garnet,—had died out. It was only a dead, cold stone!

Blanche, at the request of the hidalgo, took the young heir home with her, where he remained until he was old enough to be placed at school.

Very deeply Blanche mourned for her sister, but when at last a little one was placed in her arms, with the sweet mother-love came back the sunshine to her heart. Then other children gladdened her as the years rolled swiftly by.

    *   *   *   *   *   *   *   *

In the garden sat Alberto and the mother,

Blanche. Up and down the shaded path walked their handsome nephew, now a man grown, holding by the hand his beautiful cousin, the timid, blushing maiden Blanche.

".Do you remember, love?" said the mother, Blanche, looking fondly at the young people.

" Yes, I remember all, dear wife," replied the father, Alberto. In their walk the children came toward them, and kneeling down before them, said: " Dear father and mother, we love each other, give us your blessing."

With tears of joy glistening in their eyes the happy parents blessed the beloved children. Upon the mother's hand, in the light of the glowing sunset, shone the talismanic pearl, clear, white and shining as the purity and love within her heart that had made all her life so beautiful and happy.

FRANCETTA.

On the banks of the Lake of the Lules grew a stately palm tree. Under its shadow in a little cane hut, lived a very poor Indian woman with her five little children.

There were other trees around, but none were so beautiful as the palm, and the Indian mother loved it dearly, because in the golden days of her youth, she had listened to the pleasant story of love under its waving branches, and there in the little cane hut she had lived with her handsome white husband, and been happy, and there all the little ones were born.

Then the sunlight danced through its broad leaves, and filled the little home with warm, glowing light, and the mother's heart was so full, that its soft radiance shone from

her gentle eyes, and played around the
curves of her pretty mouth.

But that was all past. The father had
gone far away to the east, and for years there
came no word or token. So from the mother's heart all the sunshine had died out,
and though it still shone through the glittering leaves of the palms, only the children
absorbed it. It was six long years ago since
the husband had left the pleasant summer-
land of Southern California, six weary
years to the wife who, morning and evening,
had watched for his return. In her untaught way she loved him with a passionate
devotion, that is a stranger to many a cul-
tured heart.

Sometimes she would take down her long
glossy hair and sit upon the ground weeping
for hours. She could never forget. No!
hers was a real affection.

" He has gone home, the beloved father,

to the great Spirit," she would say to the
little ones, as the lonely night came on. " He
is a star in the bright Heaven. He will not
forget us, for we are his own."

Often, after the children were sleeping in
their sweet innocence, she would go out under
the palm tree, and with her eyes roaming
over the whole sky, she would find the
brightest star.

" It is his," she would say, " for he was
greatest and best of all; not even the great
chieftains of our tribe could compare with
him." Of the children, the three boys were
like the mother, inheriting the dusky complexion and all the wild instincts of the
Indian race, but the little girls were more
like white children, especially Francetta, who
was as beautiful as the brightest wild flower
of the forest. Marie was not even pretty.
She was a little sad-faced sickly child, who
had been born after the father left, and that

was reason enough that she should not be beaming and fair, yet to her little wizen face was given a rich vail of waving hair, that a princess might have envied.

Of Francetta, the mother was very proud, for every one who saw her stopped to look again, and said, "how lovely she is, and what a pity such a little fairy should live only in a cane hut, with a Indian mother."

"What a pity, indeed, my princess Francetta," thought the mother, sadly, and she would gladly have gathered the sparkling dew drops to bind about her darling's brow, but they were too fleeting. She had only coarse food, and the poorest garments, to give to the dainty maiden.

For Marie she wished nothing better, yet her fondest love went out for the little weakling, and, as the mothers always will, she cherished with tenderest solicitude the helpless child.

4

When Francetta was ten years old, she had never worn a shoe upon her pretty foot, nor a gay colored shawl upon her head, such as she has seen the Spanish maidens wear at San Gabriel. "If I only had these fine things," she thought, "I should be a grand lady, and people would say Doña to me, which is what I wish. One does not like to be only Francetta to any one who pleases to speak."

Into her heart the ripened seed of flattery had fallen, and it was growing up the great rank weed of pride. Thus it became a "great pity," not that she lived in the little cane hut with the fond Indian mother, but that every one said, "What a beautiful child."

In her sorrow the mother had become a Christian, and this was a great comfort to her; so in rain or sunshine she would send the little girls to the old mission church to mass, and to Sunday school to be taught by the reverend padre and the good sisters.

One morning the padre came to the hut and told the mother it was time for the little girls to be confirmed, and that she must send them every day to the mission that they might be prepared for the holy ordinance when the bishop came again to the mission.

The old padre sat under the palm tree, and the sunshine glistened upon the smooth crown of his head, for it was shaven closely.

He called the little girls to him, and talked very kindly to them of the Holy Mother, the Blessed Christ, and the pleasant mansions of " our Father, who art in Heaven."

Marie stood by his side, full of wonder and gratitude, looking up into his face and thinking, how happy she was that all her sins might be washed away by the blood of the merciful Christ, who had died for her, and that up in the shining heaven the loving

God would receive her just as readily as
if she had been the rich señora's child, in-
stead of the ugly little daughter of the
desolate Indian mother.

Into her eyes the padre looked and smiled.
"You understand me, child," he said.

"I do not know much, holy padre," answered Marie, "only that God is as forgiv-
ing as he is mighty, and that for Christ's
sake he will wipe out our sins from the great
book where every thing is written."

"Yes," said the padre, "you understand,"
and he went on telling more and more of the
pleasant story of God's love.

Francetta, too, stood by the padre's side,
thinking earnest thoughts, but they were not
like Marie's.

She looked at the padre's soft white hand,
and thought it much nicer than the mother's
rough palm, and at the polished boots and
glossy hat, and wondered why God gave all

these to him, and made the mother so poor.

She did not hear his kind teachings, she was so intently thinking, but when he said, "and you, Francetta, do you understand as Marie?" she answered, "yes, padre, I understand;" but the padre could not see it in her eyes, and was not well pleased with her. He talked to the mother for a short time, and then blessed them, and went away. "You will try, my Francetta, to turn your heart's eyes to the shining heaven," said the mother softly. "There in the fleecy clouds I often see such wonderful things, and God blesses me."

Francetta did not answer. She pushed away the mother's hand which rested upon her arm, and a sullen, dissatisfied frown cast its dark shadow over her brow, but upon Marie's ugly little face there was a soft subdued light that rose from her thankful heart. She only saw the tear gathering in the mother's eye, and kissed it away.

The next morning the sun shone with the fair rosy light, covering the distance with a rich purple haze. The air was fresh and pure, and there were birds with beautiful plumage in the trees, but among them sat the gray mocking bird, and sang the sweetest of them all.

The young girls went to the spring and washed their faces in the sparkling water. How fresh and rosy it made Francetta look, and even Marie had a little tinge of color upon her cheek; then the mother called them, and began to comb their long hair. Marie's she left floating about a heavy shining mass, but Francetta's she wove into long glossy braids. Poor Marie! her shoulders were high and rounded, and her frail form was very imperfect, but the luxuriant hair would cover all, and the mother's pitying love cast it over her like the sweet mantle of charity.

Dear innocent child! how often the rough, healthful children would mock at her, and call her the "ugly little hunchback," and laugh in their wild gleeful way, till her sensitive heart would throb and beat with painful timidity. Then she would run away and hide herself in the orange grove, and weep, till in the fresh air, with the bright leaves, the fragrant flowers, and singing birds, she would forget all her sorrows.

Once the señora said, "poor Marie has wonderful hair."

"Yes, Señora," answered the child, "the loving God pitied me, and made it grow to hide me from the strong handsome children who only laugh at me."

How very different was Francetta.

The graceful little maiden was light as a fawn, and beautiful as Cinderella in the ashes. Young and poor as she was, she had already learned the power of the magic spell of beauty.

All the boys and girls liked her better than Marie though she was not half so kind and obliging, and she knew it was because she was so gay and fair, while Marie was quiet and ugly. She had brought a bunch of scarlet flowers and shining green leaves from the brook, and these the mother twined into the tresses of her dark hair.

A painter would have been enchanted with the rustic little maiden as she stood under the ancient palm tree, without shawl or shoes, but that was her great trouble.

The mother kissed them, and they started on their way.

Francetta would go down by the lake. It was her mirror, and she wanted to see the bright face reflected there.

As she looked into the clear waters she

was quite fascinated, and nodded to the rosy nymph, who nodded back to her, shaking her dainty head and laughing.

Francetta brushed back her hair a little, and added another flower, saying, "Now you will do, there is no one like you, not even the señorita, and you will see wonderful things one of these days." Then she kissed her little brown hand to the water maiden, and ran after Marie, who had walked quietly on.

She was just entering the great vineyard as Francetta overtook her. How beautiful were the rich purple clusters among the green leaves, and how delicious they tasted to the little maiden warm with running. Beyond was the orange orchard white with fragrant blossoms. There were fruit trees of all kinds that the luxurious climate produces. The lime tree with its shining leaves, the rich pomegranate and the trail-

ing citron. The warm sunshine kissed
the fruit and flowers, and stole into the
hearts of the young girls; so they were
very happy, and talked in a pleasant, sister
ly way until they reached the mission.

They entered the quaint old Adobe
Church, and joined the class assembled to
listen to the teachings of the padre.

The eyes of Marie wandered to the pictures of the saints upon the wall, but most
of all they rested upon the benign face
of the Blessed Christ painted upon the great
window in the chancel.

In the light of her uncultured mind and
fervid imagination the beloved face smiled
upon her, and the voice of the good padre
seemed but the echo of the words of the
merciful Redeemer sounding from far off,
down the dim corridors of time.

Her hands were crossed upon her bosom,
and a ray of golden light from the stained

glass window, softened and subdued, fell upon her forehead.

In the shadow sat an old Indian woman listening and watching the halo that glowed upon the brow of the gentle child.

"See," said the old woman, whispering softly to her companion, "A miracle! the Great Spirit is making *la Coma Beanca* a saint."

All this time Francetta was looking wistfully at the fair little daughter of the great señor.

The señorita was sitting by her side, with her dainty feet upon the hassock just where Francetta could not help seeing them. What shining shoes encased them. About her head she wore a shawl light as gossamer, with laces and fringes, and her dress was the finest India muslin.

Her pure oval face was a very pleasing sight, but Francetta said to herself, "It is

all owing to the shawl. This proud señorita
is not so beautiful as I am, at least so says
the lake. If I only had gay shawls, rings
and shoes, one might take me for a princess
as I am. My grandfather was a great chief,
and I have good blood, which the señora
thinks makes up the whole.

Francetta was getting very much dissatisfied. Her red lips pouted, and the ugly
shadow which had stolen into her heart
looked out at her eyes and covered her
whole face. Just then the little señorita moved her tiny foot, and touched Francetta's, brown and bare, with the toes spread
wide apart. The gentle pressure of the
pretty satin shoe, bound with gold morocco,
could not have hurt Francetta, but it made
her still more angry, and she jerked her
own foot away, and great beaded tears
rolled down her cheeks. The young maidens of the class thought they were peniten-

tial tears, and that the padre's admonitions were sinking into her heart.

"Francetta understands, she is ready for the confirmation," whispered the señorita; but of all the padre had been saying, she could not remember one word. She was thinking only of the gossamer shawl and the gold-bound shoes.

Thus it was in the church, and when they passed into the sunshine, still she thought of the señorita's fine clothes, and envied her.

In their walk home, Marie threw her arms around her sister's waist, saying, "Was it not glorious in the church? I am sure the blessed Christ was there with us. He saw your tears, *hijita nea*, and will bless you."

"Do not talk to me, Marie, you are worse than the padre. You disturb me; I am thinking;" and away ran Francetta to the brook. Only the water-nymph, the fair maiden of the lake of the Tulees, could please her.

Marie did not follow her; she felt that her sister wearied of her company, but she did not think it strange. "It is no wonder," she said to herself, "I am not bright and sparkling like Francetta, but I am sorry she will not listen to the good padre." Alone she went through the vineyard, and the pleasant orchard, all shimmering in tropical light. "How delightful is the green earth, where we may live for a time," thought the child, "but Heaven, with its gates of light, is fairer still; there we may live in the glory of God's presence forever."

On the borders of the lake sat Francetta, under the great lime tree's shadow. All around were other trees and shrubs that were reflected in the clear water, and in the midst sat the maiden ; so that withal it was a very pretty picture.

In looking into the water, Francetta saw only the ugly clothes, and wondered how things could happen so strangely in this world.

Just then a queer little old woman, with a brown wizen face, came tripping along under the lime tree. Francetta was so busy with her thoughts that she did not see her, till she trod on the little bare foot with her high-heeled boot, studded with sharp nails.

Francetta gave a cry of pain.

"You should wear shoes, as I do," said the old woman, clapping her bony hands, and laughing heartily.

"But I have no shoes to wear, and you have no right to step on me," said Francetta, angrily.

"I will tell you what you shall do, my pretty child. Run up the stream a little, and on the bank you will find gold-bound shoes and a gossamer shawl. It is where the witch-hazel grows. Break a long rod, and bring it to me, and you shall have all the fine things you find under it. Keep in the shadow, mind, and run softly, or old Nickey Bend will get you."

Francetta did not wait to be told twice, and under the witch-hazel bush she found the bright gossamer shawl and the gold-bound shoes.

She took them up eagerly, and breaking a rod from the bush, started to return to the old woman. Just then she heard a merry laugh, and looking up the stream she saw the little señorita and her Indian maid wading in the water with their bare feet upon the golden sand, and their uncovered hair floating loosely in the wind.

Then Francetta ran softly back, keeping in the shadow, as the old woman had told her.

FRANCETTA.

She gave the rod to the woman, who grasped it eagerly, saying, "It was not permitted for me to gather the talisman, but you have done it well, and shall be rewarded."

She fastened the boots upon Francetta's feet, saying, "They fit you nicely, the gold-bound shoes."

The shawl she threw over the maiden's shoulders. "It is light as a bird's wing," she said, and touched it with her wand. Sure enough, it seemed like the gay wings of a bird fluttering to and fro on Francetta's shoulders. Then the old woman touched the gold-bound shoes, and they became so light that they rose from the ground, and the bright wings fluttered, and Francetta was floating along in the air. By her side was the old woman holding on to her, and bearing so heavily that poor Francetta felt she could not endure it long.

"Oh, this is fearful!" exclaimed the child, "you are so heavy I cannot carry you. Let me go back to the church to the good padre; let me go home to the dear mother."

"Hush! pretty child; think of the fine clothes; besides they are the señorita's, and every one will despise you."

Francetta thought it was all over. She could not go back, and she tried to think of the beautiful clothes, but she could only wish she had never seen them.

The old woman laughed and sung wildly. To Francetta it seemed like the shrieking of the black night-bird, shaping its shrill voice into words:

> "Here we fly through the air,
>   La-ra la-ta! La-ra-la-ta!
> A wizen witch and maiden fair,
>   La-ra-la-ta! La-ra-la-ta!
> Fine fringed shawl and shoes of gold,
>   La-ra-la-ta! La-ra-la-ta!
> Thus we're bought and thus we're sold!
>   La-ra-la-ta! La-ra-la-ta!

The chorus was terrible, it was so shrill and loud, and the old woman brought her mouth very near Francetta's ear.

"Don't, don't shriek so loud!" cried poor Francetta; "only let me go home; take the shoes and shawl. Let me go home with my bare feet and uncovered head"

"No! no! I cannot take the fine clothes. It was you who stole them from under the witch-hazel. They are the señorita's, but you must keep them now, and you shall never forget, for you stole them. They are the señorita's."

The old woman screamed this out so wildly that it seemed to pierce Francetta's heart with a sharp pain. She put her fingers in her ears, but she could not shut out the sound.

Then she tried to pull the shawl off, but it had changed into wings that were as fixed as her arms, and little wings had grown out of the heels of her shoes. She was getting very tired, but still she was forced to go on bearing her weary burden, till the twilight wrapped its gray mantle about them.

" Pretty shawl ! pretty gray shawl of mist and darkness !" said the old witch.

" Now, my little carrier-dove, we will stop." She touched Francetta with her wand, and they sank down slowly and softly upon a hill called the *Cerro de la Campana*, the hill of the bells, because its rocks when struck together sounded like the notes of bells. Yet these notes formed words, and were always the echo of the listeners' thoughts. To Francetta they talked continually of the gossamer shawl and the gold bound shoes, which, sleeping or waking, had become torture to her.

Then they would talk of the mother standing ever in the door of the little cane

hut, watching and waiting in her new sorrow, with Marie weeping by her side.

Then the bells would sound a note of half-
forgotten memories of the years gone by
before she had sighed for the beautiful
clothes, and that seemed the saddest of all,
for then she had been a truthful, innocent
child.

Very wearily she lay upon the ground,
while the old woman struck the stones together, saying, " Pretty music ! Pretty
music!"

At last she grew hungry, and touching
Francetta with her wand, told her to come
into the house and prepare supper.

Looking round, the young girl saw the
entrance to a cave, and this was the home of
the wicked old witch. Gathering a bundle
of fagots she entered the cave. From the
top were suspended curious pendants,—crys-
tals, long and slender, and covered with

shining bugs that danced over them with
their changeful light. Scattered all around
were luminous stones, like those she had
seen the grand señora wear; blue, green,
amber, and the pure light-beaming white,
which is richest of all gems; fire flies
gleamed in the recesses, and far in the distance flitted the fitful light of the will-o'-
the-wisp. It was a strange place, and so
thought Francetta as she kindled the fire of
dry fagots and prepared the old woman's
supper, who ate ravenously, while the young
girl served her.

After she was done she gave the little
maid the crumbs that were left, but they
were so few that the child was still very
hungry.

She was angry with the old witch, with
herself and with every one.

"If God is so good," thought she, "why
could he not take care of me, and give me

everything pleasant and delightful as well
as that proud señorita, who is no better
than I am?"

Every now and then the old witch struck
the sounding stones, and over and over
again they echoed Francetta's wretched
thoughts, till from great weariness her
heavy eyelids fell upon her tear-stained
cheeks and she slept.

Very early the old woman woke her the
next morning to prepare breakfast, which
the witch ate, leaving again only a few
crumbs. Then she began amusing herself
by striking the sounding stones, first touching the child with her wand. In that way
they could both hear the same echo.

"If God is so merciful, why does he not
take me away from the terrible old witch?
Why does he permit her to torture me? I
was not to blame about the gossamer shawl
and the gold-bound shoes." So echoed the

wonderful stones, for these were Francetta's thoughts.

"You stole the fine clothes, you little wretch, you knew they were the señorita's when you crept along in the shadows," cried the relentless old witch.

Poor Francetta! All daylight was nothing but hard, hard work; the cruel witch and the magic stones were an endless torture, and at night she went worn and hungry to her bed of husks.

It was a most miserable life, and for days and weeks Francetta was sullen and angry. At last, one weary night, when her limbs were sore and chilled and she was famishing with hunger, she wept bitterly, saying: "It is sad, very sad; yet I deserve it all, for I am a great sinner." Then she clasped her little red hands together and prayed,—"Oh, Lord Christ have mercy upon me! have mercy upon me!" A peaceful quietude stole over her and filled her whole heart, and she slept calmly, dreaming innocent, happy dreams.

From that night she was penitent and subdued, and the sweet mercy of the Blessed Christ fell like heavenly dew upon her chastened spirit.

One morning the old witch called her earlier than usual.

"I have a long journey to take," she said, "and you must go to serve me. Make haste, for before the sun rises we must be off."

Francetta prepared the breakfast and attended to all her duties, but before she had eaten the crumbs, the witch fastened the gold bound shoes upon her feet, threw the gossamer shawl upon her shoulders, and touching them with her wand they rose up into the air, the old witch clinging to the child as before, and bearing heavily upon her.

They went on hour after hour, till the sun seemed like a great ball of fire, burning with tropical fierceness. Francetta was faint with hunger and fatigue, and again in her great agony she prayed, " Oh, Lord Christ, have mercy upon me, have mercy upon me!"

Just then they were passing over the familiar old mission, and from the open windows of the adobe church, the penitent maid heard the rich tones of the organ and voices of the choir singing.

How delightful it seemed, and with an intense longing, she desired to kneel once more in the holy place. Again she prayed, "Oh, loving God, forgive my sins, for Christ's sake have pity upon me a miserable sinner."

Just then a great wind swept by, tearing the old witch from the child, and wrapping her in the mist of a black storm cloud that was sweeping onward to the sea.

She shrieked wildly in her frantic madness, the wailing of the wind mingled with her cries, but in the church all was a blissful quietude, and only the music of the organ and the voice of thanksgiving was heard.

Francetta sank gently down through the troubled air till she rested upon the church steps.

The evil spell was broken, but upon her shoulders remained the gossamer shawl, and on her feet the gold-bound shoes. These she must bear as the token of her repentance.

It was the day of the confirmation, and Francetta saw all the young maidens robed in white, and looking as pure and good as the pictured angels.

Marie was there, and the señorita, sitting side by side like loving sisters.

The young girl did not envy them, she was too penitent and sad for that, yet she thought it would be delightful to kneel in the sacred presence.

Bearing the folded shawl and the shoes in her hand, she crept softly forward and knelt down, bowing in deep humility in an obscure corner; absorbed in the great beauty of the confirmation service, no one noticed her, and that was a blessing.

At last it was all over. The bishop had rested his hands upon the young heads and blessed them, and they had gone out into the pleasant sunshine, while the organ pealed forth its glorious thanksgiving. The music ceased and the church was closed. Only the little side door was open, and only the kind old padre remained.

Then Francetta came trembling from her hiding place and confessed all, even the wretched thoughts that the stones had echoed.

She laid the shawl and the shoes at the padre's feet, and for Christ's sake she knew that her sins were forgiven.

It seemed very kind and pleasant of the old padre, as he took her hand and led her through the vineyard, and the orange orchard, to the dear old home in the little cane hut under the palm-tree.

When the sun was painting all the west with crimson and gold, filling the great leaves of the palm-tree with the last glorious light of the day, he gave her back into the arms of the Indian mother.

"I thought you too, my Francetta, had become a star, but the great Spirit pitied me and gave me back my child," said the mother, weeping for joy.

Then Marie came, and the brothers, and they all kissed her and rejoiced over her. Never was she so loved or so happy before.

Another year passed, and in a white robe Francetta sat among the young maidens for confirmation. She had grown in beauty and goodness so greatly that every one loved and admired her, but above all, the grand señor's son, who, when she was fifteen years old, asked her hand in marriage, for in all the world he thought, " There is no one so good or so beautiful as the Señorita Francetta.

In due time they were married, and the great mansion which in her childhood had seemed like a dream-palace became her home.

Marie! dear, good Marie! as she passed from childhood toward the golden hued gate of youth, grew strong and handsome, so that her luxuriant hair was no longer needed to hide her defects of form. She, too, married a rich and brave hidalgo, and in her home lived the dear old mother. Thus in virtue and goodness, they enjoyed the riches of true happiness through long and pleasant lives.

*DOÑA MADELINA.

AT Santa Cruz, in the good old days before the gold seekers flooded California with the spirit of wild adventurers, lived a poor old fisherman in a little cottage by the sea. It was a pleasant spot, where night and day the music of the waters fell dreamily upon the ear of the little Madelina, his granddaughter, who thought there was nothing in the world so full of beauty and mystery as the great Pacific.

Often she would tell the old fisherman curious stories, and when he would ask, "Where did you hear that, daughter," she would laugh and answer, "The breakers with their white lips and laughing voices told me." Then she would dance along, light as a fairy, singing songs so wild and

clear that the little Mexican children ceased
their careless play to listen to her, while the
old man would shake his head and say to
himself: "Was ever there such a strange,
winsome child as my pretty Lena?"

After spending all the morning upon the
bay, the fisherman would take his basket
upon his arm, and go to the mission of Santa Cruz to sell his fish to the padres and
wealthy Spaniards who were transforming
that pleasant country into rich vineyards
and beautiful gardens.

The climate of Santa Cruz is one of the
most delightful in the world, and there all
kinds of rare fruit and flowers grow with
the greatest luxuriance. The warm, rich
earth is the gentle mother that nourishes
them, and they need little care from their
foster-father, man.

Old Pedro had twined a grape-vine over
the door of his cottage, and in the vintage

season the purple clusters hung so low that the pretty Madelina could reach them easily with her little brown hand.

She was about twelve years old, and a dainty maiden for a fisherman's child. Her hands and feet were small enough for a high-born señorita, and her soft olive complexion was clear as the dawning, with crimson blushes stealing through. Her skin was like satin, her hair long, black and wavy, but her large, dark eyes were the liquid mirrors of every varied emotion. They were of a soft brown, in moments of tenderness vailed with a mist like the haze of autumn, but black and flashing with fire when fiercer passions controlled her.

Though Madelina was so young, she was quite a woman in her ways, as much so as maidens of sixteen in colder climates. The grand señors at the mission took off their plumed sombreros and bowed low to the

6

beauty of the Doña Madelina, for so they called the poor fisherman's grand-daughter.

They were brave hidalgos, and she far below them in birth and station, but beauty is a crown, and every maiden who wears it a queen.

Madelina had never been to school a day in her life, but she possessed that womanly intuition which, even in little girls, is a fairy mantle to cover ignorance and guard against bad taste in manners and conversation.

Her mother had died at her birth, but her god-mother had been very fond of her, and delighted to supply the little maiden with gay dresses and shawls of delicate fabrics, suited to a Southern clime. Madelina would deck herself in the picturesque costume of her native land, and look as beautiful as a princess of fairy land. Her short skirt displayed her tiny foot, her fringed bodice her daintily rounded form, while she wore her shawl with true Spanish grace and coquetry.

One sad evening, as old Pedro was returning to the cottage, a sudden faintness blinded him so that he caught his foot upon a rolling-stone, and fell heavily on the ground. The twilight came on, but still he lay motionless and insensible.

Madelina had placed the supper upon the table, and was singing as light-hearted as a bird; but at last, weary of waiting, she threw her shawl over her head, and ran out to meet her grandfather.

As she came to the sea-shore the voices of the waves silenced her song. There was something so sad in their melody. All the time they repeated the same words to her:

> "Doña! Doña Madelina!
> From the groves with sea-weed greener
> Than the fields of golden land;
> See we shadows round thee gather,
> Darker than the wintry weather
> Casts upon the yellow sand."

" It is silly to listen to them," she whispered, " the cruel waves are trying to
frighten me. I wish grandpapa would come!
'Tis getting dark, and the trees hold out
their long arms to me! The ugly rocks
make faces! And the cruel waves will sing
nothing, nothing, but this sad refrain :

> " Darker clouds around thee gather
> Than in cruel wintry weather
> Hovers o'er the golden sand."

The clear eyes of the young girl dilated
with startled timidity in the gathering twilight. She could not go back alone without
the dear grandpapa. So she went on till
she came to the spot where he lay so very
silently upon the yellow sands of the sea-
shore.

Just then the white light of the moon
shone out and fell upon the old man's face,
so very pallid and wan that a chill of terror
froze poor Madelina's heart, so that for a
moment she could not move or speak.

There she stood, with form bent forward, terror-filled eyes, clasped hands and blood-less lips, while in her ears, like the moaning of a dull, heavy pain, came from the sor-rowful voice of the waters:

" On the lone sea-shore,
   Where the breakers rave,
Lies the fisherman cold,
   And the pitying wave
On the golden strand
   Shall moan and weep:
' He lies too still
   In his chill, deep sleep;
He never can wake
   From his dreamless sleep.' "

The young girl sank down by the old man's side, transfixed by her great anguish, and how long she remained there, she could never tell. It seemed hours. The memo-ries of her whole life with the dear old grandfather filled her mind and heart. She thought of all the pretty pet names he used to call her, and how, years ago, when she was " baby Lena," he would carry her over the sharp stones in his arms, taking her little bare feet in his hands very tenderly. Once she disobeyed him, and when he called her and said, kindly, "Has my child forgotten what grand-papa told her?" she answered stoutly, "I did not forget. I did not do wrong."

A deep, crimson flush covered her whole face and neck. The grandfather looked very sad, as he said, "It would grieve me very much if my little Lena should not always tell the truth." Then she threw her arms round his neck, sobbing, and confessed all; and he forgave her so kindly, with a tear in his eye, half of joy, half of sorrow, and they knelt down together and prayed the " good God to have mercy upon a sinful child, for Jesus Christ's sake! Amen!"

All this and much more passed through the mind of Madelina as she knelt upon the sanded shore, motionless and tearless, gazing upon the dear pale face. She was utterly stunned by her sorrow, so sudden and unexpected.

As the wind rose, the ceaseless voice of the waves took a wilder, sadder wail:

> "Cold and dead! Cold and dead!
> Lone is Doña Madelina!
> Golden sanded shore his bed!
> Lone is Doña Madelina!"

She knew that the voice of the waves told her truly, yet she did not move or weep. She could only kneel there, looking amazed into the face of her great sorrow, dreaming and listening to the voice of the waters that would not cease.

Thus it was, she did not notice the approach of the young Don Frederico, son of the proud alcalde.

As he rode towards the mission, in the pale moonlight, he saw the Doña Madelina keeping her silent watch.

Hastening to render all the assistance in

his power, he took the old man in his arms
and carried him home. Madelina followed
silently, making no reply to his kindly spo-
ken sympathy.

"I must bring tears to her eyes, or she
will be crazed with this sudden grief,"
thought the young man, as he looked at
Madelina's pale wan face and strained eyes.

They entered the cottage, and he laid the
old man upon his bed, then turning to Madelina he took her fevered hand in his, and
spoke softly :

"Poor little Doña Madelina, you're alone
now! I'm very sorry for you! Let me
always be your friend, though I cannot take
his place. Let me be kind to you as may
be."

There was a tear glistening in his honest
eye, and a great deal more than came of
common sympathy in his heart as Madelina
raised her face to his.

How it was, she could not tell; but she
bowed down over the hand that clasped
hers and sobbed as though her heart would
break, saying, only very piteously, "Oh,
Don Frederico! He was all in the world
to me—all! and he is gone!"

The young man smoothed her glossy
hair, and comforted her with few words but
abundant kindness. After the first burst of
grief was over he left her weeping by the
bedside, and went for assistance.

The next day the grandfather was buried,
and Madelina went to live with her god-
mother.

Poor Madelina missed the kind old father
sadly. Though she now lived in a very
pleasant, spacious adobe house, in the middle of a delightful garden; she often thought,
with homesick longing, of the little cabin by
the sea-side.

The god-mother was proud of the young

maiden's great beauty, and because she was
very gentle and good, loved her more and
more every day.

After a time, Madelina became cheerful
and sang her songs again, but never a day
passed that she did not think with great love
and fond remembrance of the dear old grandfather. Very often she would say to herself,
" I will do this because it would have pleased grandfather."

Don Frederico often made it in his way to
pass the godmother's house, and somehow or
other he always curiously happened to have
a nice basket of delicious fruits, which he
might as well leave for the good señora, or
a beautiful bunch of flowers that he would
not take the trouble to carry further. The
old woman took his presents with a smile,
for she knew, perhaps, better than the young
people themselves, his pretty gifts were all
for the love of Doña Madelina.

The alcaldesa was a very ambitious woman, and she had determined that her son, Don Frederico, should marry some lady of high birth and great wealth, and when rumor brought her the tale that he was attracted by the great beauty of the poor fisherman's granddaughter, she was very angry.

" Such airs for the low born creature to put on," she exclaimed, scornfully. " Doña Madelina, indeed ! " and the alcaldesa tossed her proud head loftily and went in search of her husband. The alcalde was as little pleased as his wife, and swore to disinherit the young man unless he should give up, what his parents termed, his foolish fancy, and marry the Doña Rita, a young señorita of good family and great wealth, but very ungraceful, and, unfortunately, not at all agreeable to Don Frederico.

The young Señor loved his mother with great reverence, and when one evening she

called him to her, weeping and begging him,
for her sake, to give up the fisherman's child,
he was very unhappy.

"You will bring down the gray hairs of
your father and mother sorrowing to the
grave. Oh my son! my son!" and she went
on weeping and wringing her hands till Don
Frederico promised not to marry without
her consent; "but, mother dear," he added,
"I can never marry the Doña Rita."

With this the alcaldesa was obliged to be
satisfied, thinking "time will bring it all
right." She dried her eyes and embraced
him, calling him her beloved son, the staff
of her declining years.

When Don Frederico went out from his
mother, he walked off hastily to a dense forest, and throwing himself upon the ground,
in the dark shadow of the great trees, he
pressed his hand upon his heart and groaned
bitterly: "Oh mother! mother! you can

never know what I have given up for you
this day! The good God gives us but one
mother, and mother dear my life is yours."

He lay for hours with his face upon the
ground, then rose and wandered all day
through the forest alone.

At night, when he returned to the mansion, he found the alcaldesa watching for
him, and going to meet her he put his arms
round her neck and kissed her forehead, saying "God bless you, my mother;" then, without another word he went to his own chamber
and locked the door.

The alcaldesa saw that his face was white
with anguish, and all through the night she
heard him pacing to and fro, with a sad, un-
steady tread. She was a loving mother,
though so proud a woman, and she wept
bitterly, but said, " I could not see my noble
son sacrifice his position so much as to wed
a poor fisherman's child."

After this, Don Frederico ceased to visit the god-mother's house, and though he grew very pale and sad, he made no complaint. The alcaldesa was very tender of him, and consoled herself saying, " people never die of love, only in romances. My noble boy will soon be himself again."

Don Frederico loved the Doña Madelina very dearly, and was wretched enough. He longed to see her sweet face again, and take her dainty little hand in his, but he vowed, as he could not marry her, he would never tell his love.

Poor Madelina! She had learned to look for Don Frederico's coming, and the lonely twilights grew very long and desolate

The god-mother grew angry, and said: "The Don Frederico is a false craven;" but Madeline answered, "No! god-mother dear. We have no claim upon him. He has been kind to us, very kind when grandpapa died, but he has many friends of his own rank. We have no right to expect anything of him."

Yet Madelina remembered, in her little foolish heart, how fondly his large sorrowful eyes had looked into hers in her great trouble, and how tenderly he said, " My poor little Madelina, let me always be your friend."

Many days passed. Still Don Frederico remained a stranger.

One evening, just as the golden sunset was melting into the dewy twilight, Don Frederico rode silently along the sea shore. The little waves raised their voices and the wind wafted them to the ear of Madelina as she sat in the grape arbor at the lower end of the garden :

> " Coming, coming, Madelina,
> In the sunset glowing sheeny,
>   Noble born, and waving hair,
> In his heart love sits a-weeping,
> Silently, but never sleeping,
> As in thine its vigil keeping,

Oh! my Madelina fair,
Like a mocking spectre there."

Madelina raised her eyes and saw Don
Frederico coming towards the cottage. All
the fresh, warm blood of her youth mantled
her cheeks and brow. Her soft, dark eyes
were dewy with delight till they met those
of Don Frederico looking upon her, so full
of sadness that for the moment her heart
almost ceased to beat. He removed his
plumed sombrero from his head, and said in
a low sweet tone: "Good evening, Doña
Madelina," then passed by, his head sinking
lower and lower till the waving plume touched the arched neck of his favorite horse.

The twilight deepened into darkness, and
Don Frederico passed away from the sight
of Madelina!

Then the god-mother called, " Lina!
Lina! come in, child, the dew is falling
heavily."

The young girl went in, and laying her hand upon the god-mother's, said, "Good night, god-mother dear, I am tired, I will go to bed;" so she kissed her and went to her little chamber that looked out upon the sea.

"Her hand was like ice," said the old woman sadly; "May the Holy Virgin and all good angels protect the child."

In the chamber towards the sea, far into the night, the voices of the waves chanted:

"Cruel clouds around thee gather,
Darker than in wintry weather
Hovers o'er the golden land."

The summer seemed like a long sad dream to the maiden. Often she wandered upon the sea-shore, making garlands of the rosy shells, and sometimes when the whispering waves sung the marvelous tales of ocean lore, she almost forgot her sorrow. She would raise to her ear the great sounding

7

shell, and listen to the story of the mermaids who dwell in the coral groves. She could see their long silken tresses floating upon the bright waters, and down in the crystal mirror of the deep the gleamings of their great beauty. She dreamed of marvelous palaces, with tall pillars and glittering halls, and the diamonds, rubies, topazes and emeralds that formed the windows, making them all ablaze with gorgeous light. Then this great false shell would tempt Madelina to leave her pretty cottage home, and the good godmother, and seek the palaces of the sea, " where you could be a queen greater than the proud alcaldesa," the shell would whisper, "for your long black hair is more soft, silky and abundant than any mermaid's under the sea."

Then Madelina would unbind her hair and let it fall about her like a great waving cloak, so thick and heavy that her pretty bodice and gay skirt would be almost covered. Her tiny feet would peep out so daintily that the admiring fishermen all said, "The Doña Madelina is no common lass, but born to be a great señora." Madelina cared nothing for their praise, nothing for the coaxing sea-shell's tempting.

"The cottage is better than the sea-palace," she would answer, "the dear good god-mother than the mermaids, if only Don Frederico would come. The holy Christ have mercy upon me, I will try to be content in that state of life into which it hath pleased God to call me." Then her eyes filled with tears, and she tried to forget how Don Frederico had said: "My poor little Madelina, let me always be your friend."

The alcalde had built a lordly mansion as nearly as possible (in this Dorado) like the old ancestral castle in Spain. Towards

G209750

the sea rose the great tower, so lofty that it excited the wonder and admiration of the simple Mexicans and Indians in all the country round. Far up in the tower was a small room overlooking the sea with its white-winged ships, on one side, and on the other, the pleasant green fields and vineyards luxurious in almost tropical beauty.

This room of all others was Don Frederico's favorite. Here he carried his books, and here he dreamed his pleasant dreams of Doña Madelina.

One night Madelina woke in a great fright. Her little chamber was flooded with glaring red light, and looking out she saw the alcalde's mansion burning with such fierce, cruel flames that it crimsoned the whole sky.

Throwing on her skirt and wrapping her shawl about her, she ran out, her little feet bruised by the stones at every step. When she reached the spot the lordly mansion was in ruins, only the great tower overlooking the sea remained, and upon one side the hungry flames were creeping up with fiery tongues.

Madelina saw the alcaldesa wringing her hands and crying bitterly.

The alcalde and all the people stood gazing up at the belfry of the great tower, their faces filled with the horror of despair.

Madelina raised her eyes, and there, helpless and alone, at that immense height, stood Don Frederico!

The whole main building had fallen, and up the remaining stairways ran the forked flames, cutting off all egress.

There was no way of escape!

High up in that inaccessible tower Don Frederico was shut off from all hope of life.

The great crowd heaved to and fro in its

breathings, but not a sound was heard, a dumb horror had seized them.

From that dizzy height, looking into the death before him, Don Frederico grew faint. Throwing his arms over his head he waved them to and fro, and would have fallen, but a clear, sweet voice rose through the night air and gave back life and strength.

'Twas the voice of Madelina!

" Don Frederico! Don Frederico! Don't give up! Unravel your stocking! and drop the thread."

Then the crowd breathed freer and took heart they hardly knew why, and the same clear voice called " a rope, man! a rope! light but strong!" Then some one brought the rope.

The little thread from the unraveled stocking came down and the rope went up.

Don Frederico fastened it firmly to one of the strong stone pillars, and while the ravenous flames rushed up on one side, Don Frederico made his perilous descent, grasping the rope with a trembling hand, and praying the good God to spare him through the mercy of Christ for Madelina's sake.

The crowd stood breathless for what seemed a long time, and then one loud, joyous shout made the echoes ring.

Don Frederico, almost exhausted, had fallen into his father's arms.

"Madelina! Madelina! oh! father, *she* saved me!"

Then all looked for Madelina, and found her lying in a deep swoon, her pretty face half veiled in her long black hair. Every one was anxious to assist her, but the alcaldesa took her in her arms, saying, "She is our daughter, the bride of our dear son, who was dead and is alive again, who was lost and is found." When Madelina opened her eyes, Don Frederico was bending over her,

saying in the dear old tone " My little Madelina! My little Madelina!" and from the sea
the voice of the waves sounded in her ear :

"Doña! Doña Madelina,
From the sea groves richer, greener,
Than the palace gardens grand ;
See we brightness round thee gather,
Like the royal summer weather
Of this radiant golden land."

Then said the old padre who loved the
young folks, " There can be no fitter time
than this to join these true hearts in the holy
bonds of matrimony."

So they were married by the smouldering
ruins of that stately mansion, their hearts
looking out into the golden dawn, and all
the assembled crowd thanking God that He
had spared the life of the noble Don Frederico to make so brave and true a maiden
happy.

THE SHRINE OF SAN LUIS OBISPO.

ONCE upon a time, a great many years ago, there lived a rich Spanish gentleman who had three daughters. The young girls were very proud and fond of show, but the father was a good christian, and determined to do all in his power to make them as devout as himself.

When he looked up and saw the sky clear and beautiful, he would say, " What a radiant place heaven must be, for its brightness is shining. through all space, making earth pleasant ; " and when he saw the flowers fresh and blooming, he would say, " The good Lord made them so fair and fragrant, how can we ever forget His loving kindness."

One day he called his daughters to him,

saying, " My dear children, though you live in a fine mansion, with every luxury around you, and your clothes are of the most costly material, I fear that you too often forget that all our blessings come from God, and that you can only reach heaven through the path of humility and repentance.

" I entreat you, my dear children, lay aside your pride and selfishness, and make a pilgrimage to the shrine of San Luis Obispo. If you see any one in need or trouble, relieve his wants and heal his sorrows, so may the blessed Christ have mercy upon your souls at last. We must all go down to the valley of the shadow of death alone; alone shall you make this pilgrimage." Then he kissed them and blessed them, and they went to prepare for their journey.

The eldest took from the closet a beautiful robe, and dressed herself like a fine lady, and taking a rich purple altar cloth, embroidered with gold, she said: "I will lay this gift, so exquisitely wrought by my own hand, upon the shrine of our lady; she will be pleased and bless me, and I shall soon return rich, prosperous and happy." Filled with these pleasant thoughts she ordered a fine horse saddled, and started gayly upon her pilgrimage.

All day she rode through pleasant vinelands, but toward evening she approached a thick wood. After she had gone on for some distance, she began to fear she would be obliged to pass the night alone under the trees, with only the black mantled sky above her, and the damp ground beneath.

She was so much afraid, that she trembled at the rustling of the leaves or the breaking of a dry twig.

"O, that I had staid at home," she said, weeping, "I shall only be lost in this dismal wood; I shall die, and I am so rich and fair,

with beautiful youth just opening its pleasures before me."

She dropped the bridle, and commenced
wringing her hands and sobbing bitterly.

"Oh! that I had staid at home, fool that
I am! would I had staid at home."

The horse walked steadily on, taking his
own course, till at last he came to an open
space, and the maiden raising her eyes dim-
med by tears, saw a tiny light twinkling before her. She hastened on and found it
shone from the window of a little cottage.

"Here," she said, "I will stop for the
night and rest, for I am fearfully tired and
hungry. I will never start again on a wild
chase like this; a pilgrimage, indeed! would
I had staid at home."

She knocked at the door, and an old man
with a snow white beard opened it, saying
kindly, "What do you want, my daughter?"

"I am a miserable pilgrim," said she; "I

am weary and hungry, give me food, and shelter for the night."

"Come in, child," replied the old man, "and warm yourself by the fire; you are welcome to all I have."

The maiden entered, and taking the only chair in the poor cottage, left the old man standing, though his limbs were feeble from age.

"I am so cold," said she, rubbing her hands and holding them over the bright blaze.

The hermit placed his frugal supper on the white pine table, saying, "I have little to offer, but come and eat. You are welcome."

"Little and poor enough," she replied, in a complaining tone, "but I am very hungry."

She drew her chair to the table, and ate till there was nothing left, and the old man served her. Then she threw herself on the

only bed in the little cottage, saying : " Pray
for me, father ; I am too tired and sleepy to
tell my beads to-night."

Thus she slept soundly till the morning
sun shone in upon her face and awoke her,
but all night long the old hermit watched
and prayed.

The morning found him worn and weary,
and before the dawning he left the cottage
to gather roots and berries for his breakfast,
for he was very faint with fasting.

When the maiden arose the hermit had
not returned, but she found a bowl of bread
and milk on the table, and a beautiful bunch
of roses. She ate the bread, drank the
milk, and placed the roses in her bosom, but
they were filled with thorns piercing her so
deeply that she suffered great pain, and
when she tried to throw them away, only
the leaves fell upon the ground, and the
thorns remained in her bosom.

Sorrowfully she started on her journey, but the way became narrow and filled with rough stones. Her horse stumbled and fell, for it was only a little footpath. Not far distant there was a broad road with tall trees shading it, and flowers growing on the wayside, but well she knew the narrow path led direct to the holy shrine of San Luis Obispo.

The broad road went far away through green fields rich in fruit and flowers, and she longed very much to taste its tempting pleasures.

"I shall reach the shrine sooner by taking this delightful road," sighed the maiden. "I can ride faster; here, I should be obliged to dismount and lead my horse, and the sharp stones would cut my feet."

So she took the pleasant path, and soon a very handsome youth came riding by. When he saw her he drew up his horse, and they

rode along together.   She told him where
she was going, and they became great
friends, but after a while they came to a
cross road.

"Here," said the youth, "we must part,
but when you return from your pilgrimage
I will visit you at your father's mansion,
and lay all my great wealth and my heart
at your feet, for you are the most beautiful
maiden in the whole world, and I love you
more than countless treasures."

He gave her a luminous diamond, saying,
"Give me, my beautiful, this purple cloth,
embroidered with gold by your dainty fingers, and I will kiss it till we meet again."

The maiden's face flushed as she answered: "It is an altar cloth for our blessed
Lady."

"You are my lady," replied the youth,
kissing her hand.   Though a tear came to
her eye, she gave him the altar cloth with a

smile upon her lips, and they parted with
hope and sadness in their hearts.

The pleasant path grew wider and more
crowded, and when again the night came on,
the maiden became bewildered, and no one
could tell her the right way, so that she
was lost in the great wide world, and never
reached the shrine of San Luis Obispo."

When the second sister began the pilgrimage, she too made herself as comfortable as
possible, and though she did not take a horse,
she managed to ride so much of the way,
that by the second night she reached the
hermit's hut, and when she knocked at the
door, he said, " Come in, my daughter."

The night air was cold, and she drew
near the fire, and as she sat down upon the
only chair, she moved it to leave a place for
the hermit, saying, "excuse me, father, I
am a poor pilgrim and very tired."

In her heart she felt sorry to have him
8

standing, and she turned away, for his long snow white beard and frail body reproached her, and again she said to herself, " I am very tired."

The hermit prepared the supper, and she was hungry enough to have eaten all, for it was but a scanty repast, but though she could not deny herself the best, she left a little for the old man.

" He is used to fasting," she said, " and I am not."

After supper she was very tired and sleepy, but she saw there was but one poor bed in the little hut.

" I am so very much fatigued," she said, as she lay down ; then she turned her head and saw the old man bending over the fire and shivering. The fitful light from the glowing blaze fell upon his snow white beard, and a tear glistened in his eye, and it touched her heart with pity.

"Where will you sleep to-night, father?" she said, softly.

"Here on the hearth," he said, pointing to some straw in the corner.

The maiden looked very sorry, but she said, "Good night, father," and the old man answered, "God forgive your sins; good night, my daughter;" then she said a very short prayer and fell asleep.

In the morning she found the sun shining brightly upon the old man's white beard and pallid face, but he did not move, and when she looked again she saw that he had fainted. She brought him a cup of water and wiped his forehead, and by and by he revived, and they ate their scanty breakfast together.

The maiden was very sad, and gave the best to the old man. After breakfast the hermit gave her a withered rose tree, saying: "If you repent and confess your sins, God will forgive you, but for a penance you shall carry about this leafless rose tree till the withered leaves grow green and the buds blossom, then shall you know that for Jesus Christ's sake God has forgiven you."

Then the holy man gave her his blessing, and with a heart very heavy and sorrowful, she went her way. Though she often wandered from the path, at last, worn, weary and penitent, she reached the shrine of San Luis Obispo. With the withered rose tree always in her hands, she watched, waited and prayed, that for Christ's sake her heart might be made white and pure as the driven snow.

When the youngest daughter started, she was dressed in coarse, rough clothes. Though she walked all the way she wore no shoes upon her feet, which were very fair and tender, so that it was the third night before she reached the hermit's cottage. She knocked softly at the door, and the old man said, "Come in, my child."

SHRINE OF SAN LUIS OBISPO.   [Page 116.

She entered saying, " Father, I am only a pilgrim and a penitent, I entreat you let me rest till morning, and at the shrine of San Luis Obispo I will pray God to bless you."

" Rest, my dear child," said the old man tenderly, for he saw the light of humanity shining from her beautiful eyes.

She would not take the chair he offered her, but said, " No, father, this block of wood is too good for me," and placing it in the corner she warmed herself, while the old man sat in the chair just in front of the fire.

After a while he rose to prepare the supper, but she would not allow him to do it. Worn and weary as she was, she spread the table, nor would she eat one morsel until she had served him. After that she ate sparingly, and having said her prayers laid down upon the straw from great weariness.

Then the old man pointed to the bed, saying, "rest there, dear child, I am used to hardships and penance," but she answered:

"No, no, good father, keep your bed; this straw is all I wish, only your blessing;" so he bade her good night and blessed her, and she slept the sweet sleep of purity and innocence.

In the morning she rose very early and prepared for her journey, but before she departed again, the old man blessed her, saying: "God's love shall never leave your heart." Then he gave her fresh rose-buds, and as she placed them in her bosom they expanded, and all that long and weary journey their fragrance refreshed her. Often she grew faint in the narrow, rocky way, but she pressed on till at last she reached San Luis Obispo.

After she had laid her offering, a meek and lowly spirit, at the Virgin's shrine, and felt the blessing descend and fill her whole heart, she rose to return home, but she saw her sister, pale and wan, kneeling before the altar.

She ran to her and threw her arms around her neck, but there was no response from the cold, white arms. The repentant sister was dead!

In her hands she grasped the rose tree, covered with green leaves and blooming flowers, and their fragrance was wafted like holy incense to the altar. The sorrowing heart, through the mercy of Christ, had found forgiveness and rest.

They carried the body of the beautiful maiden home to her father, and it was buried in consecrated ground; there they planted the rose tree, and it took root, and for many years its beautiful blossoms breathed a pleasant fragrance over the young penitent's grave.

The youngest daughter married about a

year after her return from the shrine of San
Luis Obispo. She became the mother of
good and beautiful children, and often would
gather them around her and tell them of the
old hermit of the wood, and her pilgrimage
to the shrine of San Luis Obispo.

FAR away in the mountainous passes of the gold land, was a giant flume. Through it roared and rustled the sparkling waters, rushing onward to the shadowy cañon where the miners sat and washed the surface diggings for gold. In rude cabins the hopeful men lived their rough miner's life alone, for their mother's, sisters and wives were left in "the old States, the beloved spots which they still called home."

On the borders of the gulch was one cabin, better, cleaner and sweeter than all the rest. Around it blossomed fragrant flowers, and over the porch twined thick clustering vines. There dwelt Andrillio, the black browed Chilano, his wife and young daughter Pepia, who was far the most beautiful flower that bloomed in the free air of the mountains.

All the miners who had not left their hearts in the old home, would gladly have offered them to the pretty señorita, but the Chilano had vowed that no one but a miner prince should wed his daughter.

In his eyes, nothing was to be compared to the bright, yellow gold. To gain it, he had left the old Chilian ranchero, but he had not yet been successful.

"It will come!" he would say, "it is only a question of time." A weary question it had proved to the wife, who loved intensely the broad plains of Chili and the friends of her life's sunny morning. But the old man, ever weaving gorgeous visions of the future, would picture the child of their affection a princess in the gold land.

All the miners who loved the dainty maiden worked early and late washing the rich soil for gold in the sparkling waters of the giant flume. Among them all no one was so pleasing to the señorita, as the young Americano who was so handsome and daring, but who, alas! was so unfortunate.

While the other miners gathered the shining, yellow grains from the bottom of their pans after the sand and water were swept away, poor Fred found nothing left. Yet, with a sigh for the sweet Pepia, he worked steadily on.

As he passed the Chilano's cabin he had only a bunch of wild flowers to offer to the little maiden, but she saw a world of beauty in the simple gift.

Poor fellow! his trowsers were so patched with flour sacks that it was almost impossible to tell the original color.

The Chilano always looked cross at his visits, and his dark brows met in a very savage way. The mother was sad, but Pepia blushed and smiled, though her long lashes drooped over her sparkling eyes till they half hid the beautiful love that was sleeping there. So the young man never lost hope even when the Chilano invited the rich miners to his cabin and praised them to his daughter.

At last affairs came to a crisis.

An old Mexican met with a wonderful success. In three weeks' time he took out a hundred and fifty thousand dollars in gold. Still his claim paid well, and it was agreed that he would be the richest miner in all that section, and that he would not even be able to count his money.

Pepia trembled when she saw him talking long and earnestly with her father. Then she laughed merrily, saying: "What a silly girl I am, he is old enough to be my grandfather, so of course, he can never dream of me."

One morning, as she was sitting in the

cabin door sewing and singing happily, her father came and sat down by her side. There was a shadow on his face, but he tried to speak carelessly.

"What a merry light-hearted child you are, and you are so sensible, which is better than all, for it will make you happy always."

All the light passed out of Pepia's beautiful eyes, she felt the something which she had long dreaded was really coming now.

" What do you mean, papa," she asked in a hesitating voice.

The old man turned his eyes away from her face. The sight of its fresh young beauty troubled him, but he spoke out stoutly: " It is all settled," he said, " and perhaps the less we talk the better. To-morrow you will wed the rich Mexican miner. He is now a prince of the gold land, and you will live in a palace, so it will all be very delightful.

Pepia's lips were as white with terror as the snow on the mountain tops.

"Only wait a little, dear papa," she entreated, "just a short time. Indeed it is too sudden, I cannot be the rich man's wife just now, give me a little time to think of it!"

The old man loved gold above all things, but he could not bear to see the soft bloom chased from his daughter's cheek by the cold despair that filled her heart. So he promised her yet one week to wait; and when she fell upon his neck weeping and kissing him, he promised her two weeks. At last it was decided that four weeks should pass, then, if nothing happened, to change affairs, she should go to the altar, without a murmur, the bride of the rich old Mexican. They kissed each other and the father went out to tell the gold prince how it was all arranged.

"Of course," he said, "nothing can happen to make any change, and in one month's

time she has promised to become your willing bride, but until then she desires to be
left alone.   Young girls are strange, you
know," he added, wishing to make everything seem as agreeable as possible to his
friend, and, though the Mexican was not
pleased, he was obliged to submit.

Pepia went out of the cabin into the
warm sunshine, for the chill of her heart
pervaded her whole being.   She thought of
the great plains of her native land, of the
tall grass that waved to and fro, rising and
falling like the waves of the sea, of the ancient
hacienda, of the strange old woman, her
god-mother, who, in her childhood loved
her above all others.   Then it came to
mind, how, just before she left the hacienda,
the god-mother had given her a curious
goblet of fine cut crystal, no longer than a
lady's thimble.

"This is a wonderful talisman," said the

old woman. "A fairy glass. If trouble should come to you in the distant gold land, fill it with water and call on the fairy of the stream to help you."

With this memory, the eyes of the maiden brightened, and the warm flush again tinged her fair cheek. She ran into the house and placed the goblet in her bosom, then ran out again into the pleasant air. Springing forward towards the flume with dancing feet, she sang as gayly as a bird:

> "It's not quite settled yet!
> Oh, prince of gold.
> You're far too old,
> You need not try
> My heart to buy,
> It is not settled yet."

Then a clear manly voice called out to her singing:

> "Whither are you flying,
> My bird! My bird!
> To leave me you're trying,
> My bird! My bird!
> But you I will follow
> Through sunshine and sorrow,
> My bird! My bird!"

All the rich warmth of Pepia's heart shone out in her beaming eyes and glowing cheeks. There was no chill now to make her tremble; indeed, for a moment she had quite forgotten the old Mexican, who aspired to be her lord. But soon the events of the morning came back to her.

She told all the sad story to the young Americano, who gave her, as may be supposed, a hearty sympathy.

A long time they talked together, trying to think of something to help them out of the darkness, and always Pepia said: " We must not despair, Don Frederico."

Things looked rather gloomy to the young miner with his claim, that as yet paid nothing, and the pockets of his poor patched trowsers without even the smallest bag of the miner's friend—gold dust, in them.

" I must get another claim," he said, sadly, " but here they are all taken up. I will

9

go further down the cañon to prospect. I
may strike it this time! Who can tell," he
added, fixing his eyes, full of sadness, upon
the beautiful face he loved so dearly.

"I am sure you will! Something in my
heart tells me so," replied the young girl;
this time raising her rich dark eyes, dewy
with love, to meet his.

There was so much hope in their soft
light that the young miner could not despair, and with a warm "good bye," he
rushed away to seek his fortunes further
down the cañon.

Pepia stood a moment looking fondly
after the handsome Americano, then she
continued her walk to the flume. How the
waters danced and sparkled in the sunshine
as the maiden dipped her fairy goblet in the
flowing tide. She raised it to her lips and
drank the cool delicious nectar, then she
sang in a low voice:

" Help me, Fairy of the Flume,
  Lead me where youth's flowers bloom ,
  Old age casts its shadows o'er me,
  To the light again restore me ;
  Or my heart will break in gloom,
  Help me, Fairy of the Flume."

Great floods of golden light shimmered the rushing waters of the flume, and a rich silvery resonance mingled with its murmuring melody which brought new hope to the heart of the maiden. Suddenly, with a luminous flash up rose a curious little water spout, and out of it came the fairy of the flume, all shining with dew drops that glistened like brilliants in the sunshine.

"I come," she said, "to answer to the spell of the magic goblet. Whoever possesses it I am bound to assist, but after all your trouble is over, you must give it to me, for it belongs to the queen, and she is very anxious to recover her lost treasure."

"I do not understand that," replied

Pepia; "the goblet is mine. It was the gift of a dear friend who is far away."

"I know all," exclaimed the fairy, who was really quite impatient, but as she wanted the goblet very much, she condescended to explain how at a midnight festival in Chili, an old woman came blundering into the magic ring. The fairies would have punished her but by chance she picked up the talismanic goblet, which preserved her from harm by its mystic powers. Worst of all, the obstinate old creature would not give it up, but carried it away and ever since that time the fairies had been trying to gain possession of it.

"That old woman must have been my dear godmother," said Pepia. Then she told the fairy her own story, and received the promise of assistance.

The sun was sinking to rest in the glowing clouds of the western sky, before the lengthened shadow of the young girl fell across the cabin door.

The mother sat anxiously awaiting her. She had feared to see the sweet face of her child draped in sadness, and when she entered with her rosy lips curved in bright hopeful smiles she was filled with wonder.

"They are changeful as the wind, are all women," said the father, listening to her mellow notes, as she sang an old Chilian song, while she prepared the supper.

At an early hour the family retired. The old man to dream of gold, the young maiden of love, beauty and happiness.

In the morning there was a great excitement throughout the mining camp. The restless waters of the flume had burst its barriers and overflowed the Mexican's claim. Rushing on with marvelous power it washed away the rich surface earth, sweeping down the cañon with a wonderful force.

At the earliest dawn the young American was out prospecting. To his great astonishment he saw the great flood of turbid waters coming towards him. Suddenly it became clear as crystal, leaving all the rich deposit in one place, and he heard these words which sounded like the echo of a distant voice:

"Where the waters clear and bright
Rise, oh, miner, to your sight,
Stake your claim and o'er and o'er
You shall reap abundant store
Of the shining golden ore,
Till a miner prince you stand
In the glorious golden land."

The young man was greatly mystified, but why not take up a claim in this spot as well as elsewhere. So he put up a stake just where the waters left the rich deposit, and fastened to it a notice claiming for Frederick Lanson, the number of eight hundred square feet to work, to have to, and hold for life and to leave to his heirs for all time to come. This, according to the mining laws of the gold land, was all that was necessary; and now the claim was his own.

Very soon the waters passed away and in a short time he was able to begin to work. His astonishment became greater each moment. In every panful of dirt was such an immense deposit of gold that even in a day he was growing rich.

At night he took off his old ragged coat and wrapping it about his treasure, hid it away in the hollow of a rock. He said nothing to his companions about his discovery, but that evening as they sat around the cabin fire talking of the outbursting waters of the flume, he made a strong sack to contain his gold.

Again and again, the rushing flood overflowed the rich ground of the old Mexican, sweeping away its golden store till the miners ceased to repair the flume, for the rebellious waters seemed possessed by the wild spirit of misrule.

Thus passed the week, every day adding
to the young miner's treasure till at last the
great sack was so full that he could hardly
carry it and still his claim seemed richer
than ever.

At last the morning came that was to
decide the fate of the pretty señorita. Since
their walk to the flume she had not seen
Don Frederico, as she had persisted in calling her lover in spite of his bad luck. This
was a shadow upon her spirits, still she had
great faith that the fairy had been working
all things well for them.

All the miners in the gulch had been invited to the wedding, and at an early hour
came the ugly old Mexican riding upon a
richly caparisoned horse and gayly dressed.
No one, and he, least of all, doubted that he
should soon be the happy bridegroom of the
lovely señorita.

In the inner room of the little cabin sat

the unhappy Pepia, her luxuriant hair unbound and floating freely over her white
shoulders. A young maiden, her friend,
bent gloomily over her. She had come from
a distant part of the country to be present
at the wedding, for in the mining districts it
was really a great event.

Pretty little Dolores. She was full of
earnest sympathy and affection. Pepia had
told her all about her hopes and fears, and
the wonderful fairy of the flume who had
promised to help her.

With a gentle hand Dolores combed the
abundant tresses, all the time whispering
words of comfort and hope.

The guests were fast assembling. All
around the cabin stood the miners in their
holiday shirts and trowsers. A booth of
fresh green boughs had been constructed under the pleasant shade of the waving trees.
There the ceremony was to be performed for

the cabin was far too small to hold so great a company.

Under the trees a table had been spread for they were to have a great feast. This was the first marriage that had been celebrated in the camp, and every one was anxious to do honor to the occasion.

As the hour approached, Pepia's bright face grew pale with excitement. "Look out, Dolores and tell me who has come," she whispered in a voice all of a tremble.

"Everywhere I see the old Mexican with his velvet doublet and waving plumes; and all the miners, only Don Frederico, and him I cannot see."

On the little toilet table stood the magic goblet, and with eager hands Pepia grasped it, saying, in a tremulous voice:

"Help me, Fairy of the Flume,
By the goblet's mystic power,
Help me in this fearful hour,

Save me from a wretched doom,
Help me, Fairy, help me, Fairy,
Help me, Fairy of the Flume."

Every moment the maiden's face grew paler, and a deep shadow had stolen the brightness of her beautiful eyes.

It was as though the darkness of the old Mexican's years was creeping over her heart.

In the distance a faint sound, like the rippling of water, was heard. " Look out again, Dolores," said the young girl, eagerly ; and again the faithful friend crept slowly to the latticed window.

" The miners are all there, walking to and fro, and talking together. Everywhere the plume of the old Mexican is waving. He grows impatient with waiting. The guests have all arrived, only Don Frederico, and him I cannot see."

Again Pepia clasped the goblet, crying in a piteous voice—

"Help me, Fairy, I despair!
Clouds of darkness fill the air:
By the talismanic spell,
Charms that in the goblet dwell,
Rise from out the rushing tide,
Save, oh! save a hapless bride
From old age! oh! wretched doom!
Save me! Fairy of the Flume."

Just then the old Chilano knocked at the door, calling: "hasten, my dear child, the company have all assembled, and the gold prince is weary waiting, and remember he is the richest man in all the mines. Hasten, now, my dear daughter, for the priest in his sacred robes stands under the arbor. We only wait your coming."

The young maiden tore away the band that Dolores was binding about her hair, and again the long raven tresses floated over her pearly shoulders, and fell down to the floor.

"My hair is yet unbound, dear papa," she said. "It must be gayly dressed to-day."

"Very well, my child; only hasten, and soon I will come again."

"Oh, Dolores," cried Pepia. "If he should be too late, for come I know he will. Do you not hear the waters of the flume and the voice of the fairy mingling with them?"

Dolores bent eagerly forward and listened. Sure enough, amid the sound of the waters, they heard the fairy calling :

"Give me back my long lost treasure,
And your heart from sorrow free,
Bounding with delicious pleasure
With your lover soon shall be."

Pepia was almost fainting with excitement, and with a broken voice, she cried :

" Come, oh! fairy, I implore thee!
And the goblet I'll restore thee."

"Come, daughter! come quickly," interrupted the old Chilano, at the door :

"Save me! save me!
Or I die in midnight gloom,—
Come! oh, Fairy of the Flume."

Then there was a mighty rushing sound, and the miners ran forward to look at the waters of the flume, which in a great mystical torrent were again overflowing the rich ground of the old Mexican.

" See! she is coming," exclaimed Dolores, and in at the window flew the glittering fairy.

"Look out towards the lower cañon, pretty tearful bride," she said, laughingly.

Pepia ran to the lattice eagerly, and her eyes were blessed by the most beloved sight.

Yes! it was surely Don Frederico toiling onward, under the weight of a mammoth sack which seemed taxing even his manly strength greatly. All the miners went forward to meet him, for he was a general favorite among them.

" The sack is full of gold dust," said the fairy. " The young man has a claim which shall never fail him; so he will soon be the richest miner prince in all the gold land. Now give me the goblet. The honey dew will be sweeter to the queen from her favorite cup."

The fairy seized the magic goblet eagerly, saying : "I wish you joy; now, good-bye. May you be as happy always, as you will be this day."

Out of the open window, away flew the shining Fairy of the Flume; but the young girls were too busy to see where she went.

Now in earnest, Dolores began to braid the glossy tresses, and floods of rich warm light drove the shadows from Pepia's eyes.

Without, all the miners gathered around their returned companion, and as he opened the great sack of gold dust, a loud, thrilling shout arose from every manly heart. One after another they cordially grasped his hand and congratulated him, each after his own rough miner fashion.

Last of all came the old Chilano who had been looking on full of wonder. He saw it was no use to try to stem the tide which had turned against his favored scheme. Besides he was quite satisfied that it should be so, for now the young Don Frederico was a real miner prince, perhaps as rich as the old Mexican.

"Welcome my son," he said; "Pepia will be very happy in your return."

It was not long before the young miner had exchanged his poor patched trowsers for others more suited to the occasion, and though even then he was not dressed in very princely attire, with his handsome manly face, tall, agile and athletic figure, and truly gentle manners, he looked surely one of Nature's noblemen.

Now it happened that he too was standing impatiently waiting the coming of the coy little maiden Pepia.

Again the old Chilano knocked at the door, calling: "Come, daughter, the *true bridegroom* has come, the *real* miner prince is waiting, and all the guests are calling for the bride."

This time the door of the little room opened, and beautiful, blushing Pepia came forth, her young face beaming with the brightness that filled her heart. By her side walked Dolores and the mother, who all the morning had hidden herself weeping.

The happy bridegroom stepped quickly forward and clasped her willing hand in his, and all the miners greeted her with hearty sympathy and gladness.

Under the grand old trees stood the priest in his sacred vestments, ready to perform the solemn ceremony which should unite their two lives into one forever. After the marriage came the feast. All the miners enjoyed it immensely, only the old Mexican, and no where could his waving plume be seen.

In the general joy at the return of his ri-
10

val, he had gone no one knew whither, and
no one missed him.

Everywhere happiness reigned that day;
but most of all in the hearts of the successful young miner and the Chilano's daughter.

OSCAR AND CERISETTE.

THROUGH the Golden Gate floated clouds of vapor flooding the city with a sea of mist. In the distance the gaslights glimmered dimly, with faded, sickly beams, yet everywhere the ceaseless crowd rushed onward, like the ebbing and flowing of the ever restless tides.

In the rich broad streets it was still pleasant, for on either side through the heavy plate glass windows, streamed the glowing, gorgeous light that shone upon a thousand beautiful things. The passers-by were well dressed; there were smiles upon their faces, and they were talking pleasantly, though in many languages, for they were in the most cosmopolitan city in the western world.

In the poorer streets it was quite different. There it was damp, dark and dismal enough. Along one of these ran two children, a boy about twelve, and a girl perhaps ten years of age.

Between them they carried a large basket, but it was very light, for it was quite empty. The little girl was crying, and the boy seemed sullen and angry.

"There is no use in crying, Cerisetté," he said, "for old Mother Magson will beat us, and there is no help for it; then it will be time enough to begin."

"I do not want to beg any more," sobbed the child. "The people who live in the big houses will give us nothing. They hate beggars. I am quite sure of it. I want to be like the beautiful little ladies, who wear blue silk dresses and pretty gold rings."

"Don't be a goose now," replied the boy, impatiently, "you know in Italy we were only beggars. Yet there it was so pleasant

OSCAR AND CERISETTE. [Page 112.

and sunny, the sky was blue and warm, and the rich people were princes, who did not care so much for a little money. There one could live, and be happy as the birds all the day long. But here it is so cold!" and the sun-born Italian boy shivered, rubbing his chill red hands together piteously. Into his voice had crept the deep homesick longing for beautiful, sunlit Italy.

"I do not remember so much of that," replied the girl, "but I do wish Mother Magson had left us there; it was better than this I am sure. O dear! I am so afraid of the whipping!"

By this time they had approached an old ricketty tenement house, and creeping softly to the basement window, they looked stealthily in.

There in a dismal, dingy room was congregated a motley crowd of beggars, organ grinders, "tins to mend," and all

sorts, but principally Italians. The indo·
lent *lazaroni* of the classic land seemed fully
represented.

A fire of dry sticks cast its fitful glare
over the poor folks. Some were drinking
and smoking, some cooking their supper,
while others sat wearily eating the dry bits
cold.

Conspicuous among them all was Mother
Magson, as she flew about in a fitful restless
way.

She was the landlady. These were her
lodgers, and the dismal basement, her hotel.
She was unusually out of sorts this evening.
The two little wretches that she had brought
all the way from Italy to beg for her, had
not returned with the large basket of cold
victuals. There was a prospect of a scanty
supper, and her yellow leathery face was
drawn into innumerable venomous wrinkles.'

As little Cerisetté caught a glimpse of it

in the flitting firelight, she trembled so vio-
lently that Oscar caught hold of her to
prevent her from falling and making a noise
that would attract attention.

Just then, with a rude exclamation of
anger, the old woman rushed to the door,
and the children had hardly time to hide
themselves in the dark embrasure of the
protecting alley, before she was peering up
and down the street, muttering curses upon
the little miserables who had escaped her.

Presently she went in again, and Oscar,
catching Cerisetté by the hand, whispered:
"Now is our time. I will never go in
there again. Come, and be quick!"

More softly than ever they stole away,
until they came to a turning in the street,
when they ran forward as fast as possible,
till at length, for want of breath, they were
forced to stop.

The boy had involuntarily held the basket closely clasped in one hand, but as his eyes fell upon it, he threw it from him, saying, " Good bye, old basket, this is the last for you and me."

" What do you mean, Oscar, by throwing away the basket ? Mother Magson will kill us now ! O dear ! I wish I dared to go home."

"I mean," replied the boy stoutly, " that Mother Magson may do her own begging now ; we will never go back to her, nor carry her old basket again."

" But what shall we do, all so tired and hungry ? " and again the weary child began to sob as though her heart ached sadly.

" That is always the way with girls," exclaimed Oscar angrily, but as he looked at the little sorrowful face turned to him for help and protection, he added more softly, " there, do not cry now, you know you are

my sister, and I shall look out for you, so
do not be a baby."

They walked on through the darkened
streets till at last they approached the better
part of the town, more in the light.

By and by they came to a baker's shop.
What a tempting window!—it was filled
with all sorts of delicious cakes and tarts,
and the children stopped before it, looking
in with hungry eyes.

The man at the counter called out gruffly:
" go away, you little vagabonds;" but the
good wife, who held her first-born babe
closely pressed to her bosom, looked on pity-
ingly, saying, "they may be hungry, husband. The poor little things!"

Taking a loaf from the shelf, she went to
the door and placed it in Cerisetté's hands,
which trembled with eagerness as they
grasped it.

"You are very good, lady," said the child, " we were dying of hunger."

The woman embraced her little one more closely, and a tear came to her eyes as she prayed the good God that it might never be shut out in the night, cold and hungry.

"Poor little creatures!" she said, and only for the husband she would have given them more, but she had already " cast her bread upon the waters."

Out from under the thick tangled hair, from the little pinched dirty face of Cerisetté gleamed the bright, dark eyes, dewy with thankful emotion.   Again, in her childish way, she said: " the bread is so good, and we were dying of hunger."

Oscar stood with downcast eyes. He did not speak. With the old basket, he had hoped to throw aside the begging.

The woman went in and closed the shop door. He was glad of that, and began eating the bread. It tasted as sweet to him as to Cerisetté, and very soon his poor little hungry face grew brighter and happier.

It was now late, and the children were glad to find a large dry goods' box, in which they stowed themselves snugly away, and slept until the morning.

The sun arose up over the hills, and even found its way into the shadowed street between the tall houses, where the dry goods' box stood, before the children awoke. It was very quiet there, for it was Sunday, and in the business part of thé town, and no one was stirring.

"I wish we had kept part of the bread for to-day," said Oscar.

"Let us go back to the good lady, she will give us more," answered Cerisetté. "I saw the teardrop in her eye; she was *really* sorry for us."

This was no use, for the baker shop was

closed, and they dared not ring the bells at the grand houses.

On the sidewalk sat an old apple woman. It was Sunday, to be sure, but she had five children, and no one to care for them but her.

The children stopped near the stand, looking eagerly at the fruit as only the poor, half-fed can.

" I am hungry," said Cerisetté, " and so is Oscar."

" I wish I were rich," exclaimed the old woman, choking down her swelling emotion. Taking from her bag a dry crust, she gave it to the children with two fresh rosy apples. This was not robbing her own little ones, it was only her breakfast, and she could go without, as she had done many times before. Cerisetté fairly danced with pleasure as she took the delicious fruit. It was really quite a treat, and both she and Oscar stood by the old woman's side talking pleasantly until they had finished their breakfast.

Just then the church bells rung out their clear notes, and to Cerisetté they seemed to say:

> " Come, Cerisetté, come away,
> To the church this sun-bright day.
> Join the children, do not stay,
> Cerisetté, come away."

"Do you hear what the bells say?" said the little girl wonderingly, as she looked at the old woman with eager eyes, "I think they are calling me!"

"It is Sunday," answered the apple woman, "and the bells call us all to church. I went to early mass, but I cannot go again," and she sighed heavily over her own sad thoughts.

Cerisetté stood listening, and all the while the bells were calling:

> " Cerisetté, do not wait,
> Ding dong bell! 'tis growing late.
> To the Church this glorious day
> Crowds of children wend their way."

"What curious bells, Oscar. They never called me before, though with Mother Magson one could hear nothing on Sunday only the noise, for then everybody had time to drink and fight, and I was always afraid."

"Poor little children," said the kind apple-woman, "listen to the good bells, and forget old Mother Magson, who must have been very cruel to you."

"Let us go, Oscar," entreated the child. "In the church we shall be quite safe. To-day Mother Magson will look for us, but she will never think of the church."

The streets were soon filled with people going to church, and their children in holiday attire walked hand in hand by their side.

"I am ashamed to go any farther," said Oscar, looking at their torn clothes, and poor Cerisette's tangled hair and soiled face. "Let us stop, the rich people will turn us out of the handsome church here."

"But in Italy! Oh, Cerisetté, if you could only remember the great cathedral. It was like a whole city of churches all in one, and there never was anything like the grand windows. You cannot think how beautiful they are, for they are all painted over and full of brightness, and then all around there are a thousand pictures, which I shall never see again, and the poor folks could all go in and look at them."

The boy could never forget Italy; the sunny land of his birth was the beloved dream that haunted his memory.

The sun was now shining in royal splendor, the church spire was all ablaze with light, and the cross shimmered with a rich, mellow glow.

"Look, Oscar," said Cerisetté, pointing to it, "that must be like Italy. How it glistens! That is real sky sunshine, not what creeps down to us here on the ground."

Just at this moment the little church sprite looked out from the belfry and nodded to them. "Go in," he said smilingly. "In the church the choir sings beautifully, and they have an organ. It makes glorious music, for a master plays it."

"I am afraid," said Oscar, "all the people are so grand. The ladies have on silk dresses, and the gentlemen wear gloves and have glossy hats."

"Go in," said the pleasant sprite, "the church is for the poor as well as the rich. The loving Christ is there. He has said, 'suffer little children to come unto me, and forbid them not.'" The last note of the bell was sounding. It said slowly and clearly:

"Cerisetté, do not wait,
Till it shall be late, too late!
See the portal just before,
Enter now the open door.
Angels there upon you wait,
Enter ere it is too late."

"I am not afraid now," said the eager child, her cheeks glowing, and her eyes beaming with the strange emotion.

Oscar looked down at the porch of the church. No one was there. All the people had gone in, and clasping Cerisette's hand, with hesitating steps he followed them.

The organ sounded. The door of the vestment room opened, and the choir boys, bearing the cross, and clad in white surplices, entered, singing a psalm, and behind them walked the priests, chanting in deep-toned voices.

All the people rose and joined in the psalm, and Cerisette's heart swelled almost to bursting.

"Is not that the gate of Heaven?" she whispered, pointing to the great window in the chancel. "There is the good Christ who said, let the children come to me and do not drive them away."

11

"Do not whisper now," answered the boy. He too was absorbed by the strange spectacle, but not thrilled like Cerisetté.

All through the sermon the children sat by the door, listening to words which they only partly comprehended.

At length the benediction was pronounced over the bowed heads of the worshipers. The silent prayers ended. The priests and the choir boys, bearing the cross, passed into the vestment door, singing the closing psalm. Then all the people rose up and went out from the subdued light into the sunshine.

Still the children kept their places. The swelling notes of the organ filled their ears and hearts, and then in the church alone they could feel quite secure from the dread Mother Magson.

Silk dresses brushed by them unheeded, till at last all were gone, only the pastor's wife, who waited for her husband. As she walked slowly down the aisle, her eyes fell upon the poor children, who sat by the door in their soiled and tattered garments, drinking in the organ's dying cadence.

All was now over. The music had ceased, and with a startled look, as though they were just awaking from sleep, the children clasped each other's hand and rose to go.

"Stop a moment, little ones," said the sweet-voiced woman. "Tell me who you are, and if you like to come to church?"

"We are only Oscar and Cerisetté," answered the little girl, timidly. "We are afraid of Mother Magson, who beats us, and we have run away from her, and here we are quite safe, for in the church she would never find us."

"And who is Mother Magson?" asked the lady.

Then Oscar told their little story, and the pastor came in and listened to it.

"Wife," he said, "we must look after these stray lambs of Christ's fold."

With tears in her eyes the kind woman took the children's hands in hers, and led them away to the pleasant parsonage. With motherly love she dressed them in fresh, clean clothes, and when in a short time a place was provided for them at the Home, she parted from them with regret. A warm love for the little desolate ones had sprung up in her heart.

For some time they remained at this institution, and every day they improved in mind and disposition. In the dismal basement with the wicked old Mother Magson they had left the bad habits and naughty ways that an untaught childhood and evil companionship had given them. So interesting they became with their bright beaming faces, quick intellects and affectionate ways, that every one loved them.

There came at last a sad season for the good pastor and his gentle wife. Their beautiful children passed onward from their earthly homes to the Father's mansion in heaven. Then it was that the chastened mother's heart turned for consolation to the children she had sheltered with her love, and again they were brought to the parsonage to fill the vacant places around the family hearthstone. Thus, at last the poor little waifs found a real home and warm generous love to bless them.

In the genial sunshine of happiness that now dawned upon them, they ceased to mourn for beloved Italy, and as they grew to man and womanhood, they became to the country of their adoption an honor, and to the parents who had taken them to their hearts a continued blessing.

IT was many long years ago that the Californias became known to Europeans, some time in the latter part of the fifteenth century. This was the age of chivalry, and the famous crusades of the Christians against the Pagans, who possessed the Holy Land.

Then it was that the most gallant knights of all Europe left their castle homes, their lady mothers and sisters, and, dearer than all, the fair maidens of their hearts, and went forth proudly to meet death upon the sacred plains of Judea.

When at last the wars were over, those who returned, covered with a halo of romantic glory, brought with them a wild, reckless spirit of adventure, that disdained peaceful arts and the weary toils of commerce. Just at that time the exciting rumor filled all Europe with glowing tales of El Dorado, and the weary voyage of Fernando Cortez far across the water towards the purple cloud of sunset. Many noble chevaliers were ready to seek through untried seas the golden treasures of the unknown land.

Spain abounded in adventurous heroes, to whom danger was but a pleasant excitement, and difficulties only incited to renewed effort. Among these was a slender student of Salamanca, an early companion of the famous Cortez. Ramon Capello was in his boyhood and youth a dreamer, but as the years rolled by his dreams grew tame before the strange romance of his life.

Reared in the soft climate of Salamanca, the heated breath of the South entered his heart and kindled the fire of wild adventure. Long before the down upon his cheek had

ripened into the glossy silken beard he pant-
ed for freedom to court danger.   Then came
rumors of the wanderings of his old friend,
and the tales of the distant land.   As he
listened his breath came quick and heavy,
and his dark eye flashed forth the brightness
of his cherished hopes.

It was said there was an island some-
where in the tropic seas, whose sands were
shining gold, and that the restless waves
that washed the hidden chambers of the
deep often cast up rich diamonds and pearls,
so that the circling shores glistened like the
jeweled crown of royalty.

This island was inhabited by a race of
giant women, who carried spears in their
hands, and shields over their hearts, to guard
them from surprise.

They were very wise, these giant ladies of
the olden time, for they had learned what is

seldom thought of now, that woman's greatest weakness lies in her loving heart.

As Ramon grew older he thought more
and more of seeking his fortune in the new
Dorado. He was very handsome, and all
the young señoritas of Salamanca were so
much pleased with his company that perhaps it was not strange he decided to visit
the Isle of the famous Amazons, for vanity
whispered that arrows from handsome dark
eyes would pierce the shields of the Amazons' hearts more easily than the tempered
steel of his shining lance.

It was some time before he succeeded in
obtaining a vessel and men to accompany
him on his voyage of discovery, but at last,
by creating a great excitement, he woke
the cupidity and ambition of the people so
greatly that he was obliged to refuse hun-
dreds who wished to join his expedition.

We, in San Francisco, have only to recall

the great Frazer river excitement to understand the secret of his success.

Like the return of the seasons come periodical sensations, that agitate the people never less because the last was a failure. The eager crowd are always ready to listen to tales as famous as Don Ramon's story of the golden Isle of the Amazons. Thus it was with the listening Spaniards years ago. Shares enough in the Amazon Gold Company were taken to provide Don Ramon and his followers with all they thought necessary for a long and difficult voyage.

Neither Don Ramon Capello nor any of the noble Spaniards who accompanied him, were ambitious to bring home one of the giant ladies to grace their castles. "Give us always the beautiful señoritas of our loved Spain," they said, "who know so well their duty to us, their liege lords." Capello was proud and happy as he stood upon the deck of the swift " Sea Bird," and dreamed of the unknown shore to which he was going.

He knew bright eyes were filled with tears for him, but his lips were wreathed with smiles, and the light of his eyes was as clear, bright and sparkling as the sunshine on the waters.

Thus they left the vine clad shores of castellated Spain, their hearts bounding joyously with hope, and bearing youth, beauty and strength to the conquest of the Amazons.

For many days they sailed on with winds fair and foul, and storms that woke the echoes deep down in the slumberous caves of ocean.

Through all this the sailors were staunch and true, and Don Ramon proud and hopeful. Still, months flew away, and the golden dreams of their ambition grew fainter.

Their longing for land was very intense, as they looked out into the great distance, and saw nothing but the desolate waste of waters. The light died from their eyes, the pallor of despair cast its dread whiteness over their wasted faces. The food was getting low in the larder, and a dead calm was upon the waters. Don Ramon was obliged to put the men on allowance, but he gave them pleasant words, and smiled so kindly that they all loved him, and gave a hearty "aye, aye, Señor," to all his commands. More than ever they loved him when they saw that his portion of food was as poor, and smaller than the meanest sailor's.

One evening, as the glowing sun sank beneath the still tropic sea, leaving the whole West gorgeous with golden and purple beauty, the reverent padre, Salvo Leverno, rang the silver toned vesper bell.

With one consent, there upon the deck,

the padre, the commandant, and all the ship's crew, knelt down in prayer.

The rich coloring of the sunset gave place to the sombre gray of twilight, and then to the black darkness of midnight, and still the low sad cry of prayer and penance rose from the deck of the "Sea Bird." Towards morning a slight breeze stirred the sails, then awoke the waves of the slumberous sea.

The delicious twilight of that never to be forgotten dawning, so cool and pleasant after the weeks of intolerable heat, was precious balm to the fevered pulse of the Spaniards. As the sun rose a strong breeze filled the sails, and the hungry eyes of the young Don Hortado Mendoza saw in the distance a dim purple outline that must be land.

Uttering a wild thrilling cry of joy, he roused the echoing hope in the hearts of his companions. Every eye was strained, and soon the exulting cry of "land!" "land!"

ran from the heart to the mouth of every man upon the weary " Sea Bird." Tears of joy flowed down the bearded cheeks of the hardy sailors as they saw before them the most beautiful isles of the West, the famous Amazonia.

Again the padre called them in the early morning to join in the glorious thanksgiving mass, as they sailed proudly toward the jewel crowned island. It was the burning noon-day when they disembarked, but before seeking the delicious shade with which the island abounded, with uncovered heads again they knelt upon the scorching sand and offered up a renewed tribute of thanks in their gratitude for the mercy of heaven.

All around them, upon the shore, mid sands of gold, lay glittering pearls and diamonds, but Don Ramon and his men were sick, hungry and worn with long months of toil upon the sea, and would have given more for plenty of good food and cool delicious water, than all the jewels in a monarch's crown. When they rose from their knees, dignified Spaniards as they were, they started off, running as fast as their weary limbs could carry them, towards the velvet turf and waving trees before them.

They knew there was water near, and every drop to their parched throats was worth more than all the beautiful diamonds upon the seashore.

When they reached the pleasant shade, and drank of the pure water that bubbled up from a crystal spring deep down in the dewy earth, they felt a peaceful rest stealing over them. The raging fever of their blood was cooled, and in its place came a balmy quietude, such as can be experienced only by those relieved from the suffering of extreme thirst under a tropic sky.

They had long been hungry; for forty-eight hours they had eaten nothing, but in their painful thirst they had forgotten hunger, and the water had so refreshed them that they threw themselves upon the green grass and dreamed such peaceful dreams as had not visited their slumbers since they left the shores of castellated Spain.

Hortado Mendoza was the young cousin of Don Ramon. The commandant loved the beardless boy who had followed his hard fortunes. As sleep crept softly over them, the youth rested his head on the body of his loved señor, and threw his arms fondly round him.

As he slept, no doubt he dreamed of Salamanca, for teardrops glistened under his silken lashes.

Softly he breathed the name of the fair señora, his mother, then sprang forward to embrace the dear creation of his dream. The quick motion awoke him. He opened his eyes to see bending over him one of the giant women, and his face, full of terror and surprise, reflected in the shining mirror of her shield. The boy gave a quick, startled cry, and in an instant every sleeping Spaniard was aroused and ready to fly to arms.

Their weapons of defence, which they thought to find by their side were all removed, and they were surrounded by an army of giant women, their helpless condition reflected in a thousand shields, which the Amazons carried on their left arms. They shook their glittering spears in such a relentless manner, that at least some among the gallant band who had dared so many dangers by sea and land, felt their hearts quail with fear.

These women were not destitute of beauty, but compared with the gentle señoras of the Spanish land, they were like the marvellous "Big Trees" of Calaveras, to the rich flow-

ering rose trees of our gardens.   The eagle-
eye of Don Ramon took the whole situation
in at a glance.   They were surrounded by
an army of women, to be sure, but they were
like giants, and armed with tempered steel,
while the Spaniards were few in number and
defenceless, and compared with these Amazons in size, were boys, and very small boys
at that.   Don Ramon decided, in this case
at least, that wisdom was the better part of
valor, so he brought a smile to his lips, and
filled his dark eyes with the light which had
so often intoxicatpe the fair señoritas of
Salamanca.

Going up to the most stately of the Amazons, he bowed with such a courtly grace,
and threw such an air of pleasing hmoage
into his manrne, that the giant Queen was
evidently quite taken by surprise.   She drew
her shield close to her heart, and shook her
glittering spear furiously, but Don Ra-

mon, who had often stormed the citadel of a
woman's heart before, was nothing daunted.

Again he bowed so low that his long
waving plume nearly swept the ground, and
when he raised his head he looked so fear-
lessly into the face of the giant Queen, and
threw such a bright, cheery smile upon the
shining surface of the shield, that even the
steel glowed in its sunny warmth.

Women admire nothing in men so much
as bravery, and of all things, nothing is so
contagious as a genuine hearty smile, and
before she had even dreamed of relenting,
the proud Amazon Queen had yielded to its
witchery, and given back answering smile
for smile.

When Don Ramon saw the firm lines of
her mouth grow arched and soften, he knew
that the danger was past, and when he said
in his rich full tones: "We are your slaves,
Señora, the willing slaves of beautiful wo-

man," he felt his heart beat with the pride of a conqueror.

The Amazons looked with amazement upon their warlike Queen, as she cast her shield aside and sat down upon the velvet grass with Don Ramon, kneeling at her feet, smiling and talking so pleasantly in the soft Spanish tongue.

Courtier like they followed the example of royalty, and the ground was soon all ablaze with glittering shields, but the hearts of the Amazons were left unprotected, while at the feet of each sat a gay cavalier. A great feast was made, and nothing but the sound of mirth and festivity was heard upon the island.

The fair Amazons began to use their shields for mirrors, and thought of nothing so much as making themselves beautiful and attractive to the handsome young strangers.

They would sit for hours braiding their

long tresses, and staining their eyebrows and eyelashes, so that in their dark setting their eyes shone out like the jeweled stars of night.

This change, from the toils of the sea, was very pleasant for the weary Spaniards for a time, but soon they found that, though caressed and fêted, they were prisoners carefully guarded.

They noticed with surprise that the Amazons thought nothing of the riches that lay scattered upon the yellow sanded seashore, and that the gold and jewels that decked their stately brows in so great abundance, were far purer than any they had seen, and were convinced that the rich stores of the island's wealth were kept secret from them.

One moonlight night, Don Ramon had ordered his hammock swung from the branches of two lime trees in the royal garden. It was very warm, but the atmosphere was pure and clear.

The salt sea breeze invigorated him as he lay looking up to the stars, and thinking how strange that fate should chain him a prisoner upon the isle of his great hopes.

"I am but the plaything of this giant Queen," mused he. "I, a strong brave man, am treated like a boy in leading strings. I must plan some way to escape from this bondage. True, the Queen is fond of me, and wishes me to remain always with her. She is pleased to make me her favorite, but she is far too large and the island far too small, to satisfy my ambition. I long to return to Spain, dear Spain; there one could be happier with a tortilla, a bunch of grapes, sunshine and a beautiful señorita, than to be lord of any other land. But I must go back a rich hidalgo—I must find the hidden treasure. These Amazons have gold enough, and to spare. My brave men must not re-

turn to their dear native land empty
handed.

"No one minds Hertado. These women
seem to think the boy too much of an infant
to do any harm. He alone goes where he
will unguarded. He must search for the
treasure. He shall gather flowers, throw
gold and jewels into the sea, affect the play-
ful innocent, and while the Amazons laugh
at his wayward freaks he shall make us free-
men. Don Ramon fell asleep, dreaming,
after the fashion in Salamanca, that he had
discovered a gold land so great, that compared with it, Amazonia dwindled into a
tiny speck upon the ocean.

The sun was shining through the branches
of the lime tree, and the pleasant voice of
his young cousin greeted him when he
awoke. Still lying in his hammock, he
called the boy to him, and hastily whispered
his plans. "Do you think, cousin mine,"

said Don Ramon, taking the boy's hand, "that you will be able to accomplish our wishes?"

"If you do, remember you will be a wealthy don of the old dominion, and you will merit my warmest approbation and gratitude."

The large dark eyes of the boy glistened with delight. He, of all others, was chosen for the difficult task. Don Ramon fully equaled his boyish ideas of a genuine hero, and by this standard all others were measured.

"I will not fail to find the treasure, cousin Señor. I am sure I shall succeed, and you will love me then," added he, raising very reverently the hand of his master to his lips.

"Love you! I always loved you, my boy," replied Don Ramon, embracing him. "Go now, we are observed."

Just then one of the Amazons came into the garden.   Don Ramon rose and bade her a pleasant good morning.

"You find me," he said, "caressing my young cousin. The boy is very dear to me."

Calling after Hertado, who was going away, he added, "do not forget to bring me some beautiful flowers for the Queen. You, who are so fond of rambling through the woods, must bring back the fruit of your wanderings."

"You shall have them, cousin Señor, if I have to hunt the whole island over for them."

Smilingly the Amazon said, "go any-where, my child, but over the hill on the south side. There, danger would come to you."

"Never fear," said Hertado, "I will re-member, but the Queen must have her flowers," and with a careless laugh he ran towards the jungle.

"How fond he is of our Queen," said the Amazon, looking pleasantly after him. " I trust no harm will come to him."

"Do not think of it for a moment. He will return by nightfall with the rarest flowers, and, lady fair, you shall have a share of them."

Thus the young Hertado went forth to seek for the treasure without creating suspicion.

"On the south side, over the hill," he mused, " there is danger! There is the treasure! To win it I dare anything! I am of too good blood to fear danger!" and he drew from its sheath the slender blade the Amazons called his dagger. "Yet it may be the treasure is not there; I will look everywhere else, and last on the south side;" so he wandered the whole island over, but could not find the secret hiding place.

Every evening he brought rare flowers to the Amazon Queen, which pleased her so much that she gave him the name of " Flower Child."

His wanderings had proved so harmless that the Amazon guards only gave him a pleasant salute when they saw him take his basket and start for the jungle. One morning he went earlier than usual, and walking at a rapid pace was soon out of sight, and in a few hours he had crossed the mountain and found himself in a dark ravine on the south side.

Low soft music fell upon his ear, the sweet voice of a maiden, singing to the accompaniment of her light guitar. Very cautiously he followed in the direction of the sound, till it led him to the entrance of a cave. There he saw a beautiful young Spanish girl singing to a most hideous one-eyed giant, who was dozing upon a bench just under the shadow of the tall trees that half concealed the cave. The face of the maiden was very sad, and the tears ran down her cheeks as she sung the songs of her native land.

Hertado was filled with admiration for her wonderful beauty, while her sorrows touched his heart so deeply that he resolved, no matter how great the danger to himself, to effect her release and carry her back to the land of her songs and tears. After a while the monster fell into a deep sleep, and snored so loudly that the echoes from the cavern sounded like the mutterings of a storm.

Hertado whistled softly one of the Spanish airs the maiden had been singing, and she raised her eyes to meet his, full of kindness and eager sympathy.

Though she was greatly startled at this welcome, but unexpected sight, she did not dare to speak to him, so she only held up her hands and showed a light, firm chain that bound her to the cavern.

She glanced fearfully at the giant, who was sleeping, and sang again to the same air :—

> Bring me a file to sever my chain,
> The star flower red that grows by the main,
> In the giant's broth I will let it steep,
> His slumber then will be long and deep.

Just then, much to her terror, the giant opened his hideous eye all aflame, and called out crossly " Giavota, why do you mumble without the guitar. Is your voice so pleasant that you need no accompaniment, or is it because I like the guitar? Call that singing, indeed! If I should strike you with my little finger, you would see the stars in the day time."

Giavota trembled so that she could hardly sing, but again she took her guitar, thanking the good Lord that his sleepy giantship had not noticed the words she had sung.

Hertado dropped silently to the ground, while Giavota's sweet voice rose, at first tremulously then swelled into such a rare gladsome gush of melody that Crau the cross old giant, was charmed into good nature, and as he listened with sleepy pleasure, Hertado stole noiselessly away.

That day a great feast began at the Amazon court, which was to last three days and nights.

The flower child presented his gifts to the Queen, and soon after, excusing himself by saying the heat of the sun had given him a severe headache, he retired.

After resting a short time, he went back over the hill to the south, carrying in the pocket of his doublet a file, and in his hand a large bunch of blood-red flowers.

Just as he reached the top of the mountain, he saw the giant with immense strides walking his rounds, to see that all was safe for the night, near the valley of the treasure.

Hertado crept hastily into a hollow log, and in a moment more the one-eyed monster stepped heavily over his head. He looked over the mountain on all sides, and when he became satisfied that all was safe, he went down to the sea-shore to take a bath. As soon as he had gone, Hertado came out of his hiding place, and ran to the cavern, where he found the maiden waiting for him.

He gave her the file and the flowers, and in a few hasty words they made their plans. She was to file the chain and boil the sleep charm in the giant's broth, and he to drop the mystical flowers into the flagons of Muscal for the Amazon's feast that night; then to return with Don Raymon to the cavern. They were to carry off the maiden, and as much of the treasure as possible to the Sea Bird, and with the rising tide set sail for dear, beautiful Spain, and still the homesick longings of their hearts.

It was well they were in haste, for hardly was Hertado out of sight, before Giavota saw the giant approaching, his long hair and beard dripping with sea foam, and his lone eye glaring with hungry impatience.

"Giavota," he called loudly, "you lazy baggage, where is my supper? You know I will not wait for it when I am hungry. Fly round, or I shall hurt you."

"I could get it so much quicker, only this chain hinders me," said Giavota, holding out her hands. "Take it off, and I will season your broth so nicely in a moment, and then I can serve you so much better," she added, smiling.

"I am so hungry," said the giant, "it can do no harm just till I have eaten my supper."

And he took from his bosom a little silver key, and unlocked the chain, saying, "if you try to get away, I will throw you into the sea."

"How could I get away from you, if I wished," said the delighted girl ;

"You with your long strides could catch me if I had on the famous 'seven league boots,' and I have only my poor bare feet that the stones cut at every step!" and Giavota held out her little dainty foot, bleeding and torn.

"To be sure! to be sure! I could catch you, miserable little pickaninny! But be quick, or I will eat you;" and the giant showed his great ugly teeth and grinned so horribly that Giavota shuddered with fear.

She lost no time in preparing the broth, nor did she fail to flavor it with plenty of the blood-red flowers of sleep.

It proved so delicious that the well pleas-

13

ed giant praised her, and ate till he fell back sound asleep in his chair. Then Giavota held a bunch of the flowers to his nose, so that at every breath he inhaled the essence of sleep.

"He is all right till after the tide rises, and then we will be safe, the good Lord willing," said Giavota, bowing her head and crossing herself reverently.

She found the key of the treasure cave in his doublet; and hastily unlocking the door, she selected the most beautiful jewels and purest gold, making great heaps of them for the Spaniards to gather up. There was no time to lose, she knew, and she grew impatient for the return of Hertado.

In the meantime he was not idle. He returned to the fete, and dropped plenty of the oil of sleep flowers into the Muscal.

The Amazons drank freely, but the Spaniards only touched the glasses to their

lips, so that at an early hour sleep had fallen
upon the Amazon host, and their prisoners
were hastening away over the mountains towards the south.

When they arrived, they found the giant
in a heavy sleep, and Giavota just coming
to the entrance of the cave to look for them.

Don Ramon was so much enchanted with
the beauty of Giavota, that in gazing at her
sparkling eyes, he forgot the great treasure
before him.

" Lose no time, Señor," said the maiden,
timidly, " if the giant should awaken, or the
Amazons!" and she shuddered to think of
the fate that would await them all, and especially she feared for the handsome señor.

The gentle voice of Giavota recalled Don
Ramon from his dream. He must save
her. His men should load the Sea Bird
with the treasure scattered in such profusion
around them.

He ordered every man to make haste and work with a will, while he led the beautiful maiden over the mountain to the waiting Sea Bird. All night long the sailors worked heartily, their torches fastened to their sombreros to light them on their way.

In the twilight of the morning the anchor was weighed, and the Sea Bird flew over the waters like a living creature. Just as the Isle of the Amazons was melting into the purple mist of distance, the young Hertado, looking through a powerful glass, saw the whole army of the Amazons rushing to the shore.

Tearing their long hair, which hung in tangled masses over their shoulders, and wringing their hands, they ran frantically up and down the beach, while a low, wailing echo of their cry reached the Sea Bird flying over the water.

Then came the giant, pulling up by the

roots the trees in his way, and the Amazons, turning their anger upon the treasure keeper, horrible giant as he was, drove him with their sharp lances into the sea, till the hungry surf devoured him.

Then every Amazon drew her glittering shield to her breast, and the whole shore was ablaze with light. Tradition says that the Queen published an edict decreeing the punishment of death to any Amazon who should dare to lay aside the protecting shield. Thus from the days of Don Raymon, sleeping or waking, the shield has cast its glittering light over the breast of the Amazon and over the isle of treasure, casting its bright reflection far out upon the sea.

Hertado gazed shoreward till the lustre of their shields was lost below the horizon, as fades the glow of sunset.

The Sea Bird had a prosperous voyage,

and Don Raymon became every day more enamored with the beautiful Giavota. He thought her dark eyes far more beautiful than those of the far famed Circassian maidens, and her form more exquisitely moulded than the most perfect statuary, while her rich complexion and velvet skin far surpassed the master painter's art.

They were betrothed upon the Sea Bird, and when they reached Salamanca, amid great rejoicings and festivities, they were joined in the holy bonds of marriage.

In all Salamanca there was not a braver, richer, or more noble man than Don Raymon, nor a more beautiful lady than the Señora, his wife, and they were happy in doing good.

The young Hertado received the honor of knighthood, and as much wealth as the most ambitious could desire.

Indeed, all the stockholders of the Ama-

zon Gold Company, and even the lowest
sailors on the Sea Bird were made rich, and
thus ended the expedition in search of the
jewel crowned Isle of the Amazons.

KRISS KRINGLE AND BELCHNICELL.

IN the quaint old town of Amsterdam, lived the honest Dutchman, Hans Von Armer. He was very poor, and his little hut by the big canal was more wretched than the cabin of a slave.

He and Margarette, his wife, worked very hard to provide food for four little hungry mouths, and clothes for four little frames, that, thank God, were growing in health and strength every day; but often the snows of winter came on finding the little feet red and bare, and in the chill mornings and evenings very cold and frost bitten.

At night when Hans came home from his hard day's work, all the children ran out to meet him. Frank, Karl, Ethel and baby Margarette, who was just beginning to walk and to lisp a broken welcome to the dear papa.

The mother standing at the door smoothing her clean apron, smiled upon him just as though she had not shed tears over her work as she prayed to the good Lord to have mercy upon them, and help them, and keep the cruel wolf, hunger, from their door yet a few years more ; then, with God's blessing, the boys would be able to work and help the poor weary father.

Baby Margarette was the father's darling ; perhaps because she was the youngest, or it might be because the soft light of her mother's eyes had descended to the little maiden. When she used to run to meet him, he would take her in his arms, and holding the little aching feet in his big rough hands, call her his poor little blue-eyed baby in such a pitying tone, right from his warm fatherly heart, that it would have made you sad to hear

him, and you would have felt like giving her
a pair of your warm shoes and stockings.

Even the child seemed to feel there was
sorrow in his gentle voice, as she nestled her
little face down in his neck, and smoothed
his unshaven face with her chubby hands,
calling him the dear papa, and kissing him
till he smiled and thanked God for the
baby's love. All the children would laugh
and clap their hands to see the little Margarette and the father so happy. She was such
a cunning little baby, they all thought.

Then the mother would call them to their
frugal supper, always helping the father
first; he had been a kind, gentle husband to
her, through all the dark days that poverty
had circled about their married life, and her
woman's heart, though often buried in tears,
was always seeking something to bring the
light to her beloved.

Like every true wife his happiness became her great aspiration, and no sacrifice was too great for his and the dear childrens' sake ; so, though they were very poor, and health and their love for each other was all they possessed in this world, they were often happier than many who dwelt in palaces, rich in luxury but poor in love.

The winter that Margarette was three years old was a very severe one. Early in the fall, snow and frozen sleet covered the ground, and as the year drew. near its close, the cold was intense, and heavy storms brought on the darkness while the hours of day yet lingered.

It was Christmas eve, Hans and his wife sat talking together over the fire of dry sticks the boys had gathered from a distant wood. The heat from the scanty blaze but half penetrated their benumbed forms, and the flickering shadows on the walls seemed mocking them.

Without the storm raged piteously, the rain leaked through the roof, and the frozen sleet drove in at the crevices of their wretched hut.

The rough night-wind as it shrieked through the dry boughs of the leafless trees echoed the dreary story, graven upon their hearts—the old story of hard weather, much work, and little pay; of four little hungry mouths to feed; of worn out clothes and little feet bare and covered with burning chilblains.

The little Margarette murmured indistinctly in her sleep. Hans rose and took the child in his arms, and, pressing her closer to his heart, gathered his rough coat about her shivering form.

"The dear papa," she lisped softly, and smiled, as if the presence of his love warmed her heart and brightened her innocent dreams.

Hans looked into the pure little face that

nestled so close to him, and smoothed the shining hair that, in the fitful firelight, looked like waves of gold. A tear gathered in his eye, and then another, and another, till they chased each other down his cheek, and fell upon the closed eyes of his darling.

He was thinking how light, warm and luxurious, every thing was in the stately mansion where he had been working all day long, and of the beautiful Christmas tree that looked as though it had been decked by fairy fingers.

There were toys of exquisite workmanship so expensive, that the money paid for them would have fed and clothed his little ones for the whole long winter.

He drew the child yet closer to him, and, bending over her, kissed the falling tears from her blue veined eyelids, saying, " father is sorry for his poor little baby, poor baby." His voice trembled with emotion, the future looked very desolate for him, the mother, and them all. Then the mother came and laid her hand caressingly upon his shoulder and said :

"This is Christmas eve, my husband, the night the blessed Christ Child was born. Remember, dear, he was born in a manger. The holy virgin was poor, and she will pity us. Let us bless the good God and pray that our sins may be washed away. Though we are poor, cold and hungry in this world, we may at last find perfect rest in Heaven."

Hans laid the baby in its poor little bed, and drew the scanty covering over it, and kneeling beside their sleeping children, they prayed for patience, forbearance and love in this world, and thanked God for the hope of eternal rest in Heaven the Golden.

When they rose from their knees, Hans saw a brightness in Margarette's face, that told him God's blessed light was glowing in her heart, and he gathered hope from the woman's faith and trust. · He heaped the dry sticks upon the smouldering embers, and taking Margarette's hand, drew her to the fire and began to talk cheerfully of the future.

By and by, Margarette thought she heard the merry jingle of sleigh bells, and the neighing of horses. Hans told her it was only the storm, and the wind sounding its harp through the leafless trees.

Nearer and nearer it came, and Hans said the storm was increasing. So it was; the wind blew in heavy gusts down the chimney, till at length Hans was obliged to put out the fire, telling Margarette they must go to bed to keep warm, and he would take the baby with them, it was such a fearful night. Then Margarette rose to put things in order, like a careful wife, before retiring.

The rickety casement shook in the changeful blast like a shattered mill, but above all, to Margarette's ear came the cheerful ringing of sleigh bells, saying over and over again :

"I am coming! I am coming! Cheer up! Cheer up! Kriss Kringle! Kriss Kringle!"

"Hans!" said Margarette, while the red blood rushed to her lips and cheeks, "it is the Kriss Kringle. The good Lord has sent him to us!"

And sure enough it was the Kriss Kringle.

There before them he stood, laughter covering his jolly red face from eyes to chin. Shaking the snow from his long beard and shaggy coat, he made the hut ring with his "Merry Christmas to you all!"

Then he laughed such a clear, joyous laugh, that Hans and Margarette caught the infection and laughed too, though there was a tear in Margarette's eye, for she saw all sorts of things she had wished for hanging from his shoulders, and almost falling out of his huge coat pockets.

He looked so burdened that Margarette asked him if he was not tired, carrying such a load.

The Kriss Kringle only laughed again, and told her he had carried as much to many other places; but that he must hurry, as he had a great deal to do before morning —so he began taking the things out of his pockets.

There were shoes and stockings for all; such pretty little red ones for baby, and warm dresses and coats for the children; and for the dear, patient mother a dress and just such a nice woolen shawl as she had wanted for a long time, and great coat and boots for Hans.

The tears that had at first only glistened

14

in Margarette's eyes now flowed down her
cheeks ; and she softly whispered to Hans :
"Oh ! the dear Christ Child, he washes away
our sins, and heals all our distresses. He
has heard our prayer and made the eve of
his birth blessed to us all."

Then the Kriss Kringle took from his
pocket a pair of skates for each of the boys,
and for the little girls two beautiful dolls,
with curly hair and eyes that could open and
shut.

"Oh, my little children! How happy they
will be!" sobbed Margarette, while the Kriss
Kringle laughed, and his rosy face looked
merrier than ever.

"Tell the little ones to look out for the
Belchnicell. If they are naughty, he will
come and take their pretty gifts away ! He
always watches the Kriss Kringle's little
friends, and if they are not good will punish
them!"

"How can they help being good, with all these beautiful things," said Margarette. Then she thought how often her son Franz disobeyed her, and sighed; but she hoped after this visit of the Kriss Kringle even he would try to be a good boy.

The Kriss Kringle gave Hans a large turkey and a pair of ducks as the last gift, and with his merry ringing voice again wished them a Merry Christmas and a Happy New Year.

"Do not forget the *Belchnicell*," he added, and before they could thank him, he was gone. Hans and Margarette looked at each other with wondering eyes, and Hans said:

"Did you see how quickly the Kriss Kringle went out at the window? We could not thank him;" but Margarette laughed, and answered:

"Hans, dear, the Kriss Kringle went up the chimney, but as we could not thank him we will thank the good God for all his blessings; but most of all for the dear Christ Child, and the hope of Heaven the Golden.

So they knelt down and prayed again by the bed-side of their children with hearts full of thankfulness, and when they rose up the storm was over and the clear light of the stars was shining in upon them.

Again they spoke of the merry Kriss Kringle; but all their lives long, they could never determine how he came or went away.

In the morning the mother called all the children to her and told them of the visit of the good Kriss Kringle, but before she gave them any thing, she talked to them in low, gentle tones of the dear Christ Child, and told them that all good came through him; pointing above the clear morning sky to the bright Heaven where he dwells in the Father's Mansion.

Then they all repeated together: " Our

Father in Heaven;" and she kissed them and spread out before them their beautiful Christmas gifts.

Never were four little children so delighted. These were the first presents they had ever received.

They were all very quiet and attentive while the mother was talking to them except Franz, who so longed to hold the coveted treasures in his hands that he could hardly repress his impatience.

Last of all she told them to beware of the watchful Belchnicell who, if they were naughty children would punish them and take away all the Kriss Kringle's beautiful gifts.

They promised to be good, and as she gave them their presents she kissed them, and they were very happy; for never in all their lives had they possessed so many beautiful things.

As they turned joyfully away the mother looked lovingly after them, and as her eyes rested upon Franz, a sad light filled them and again she called him to her.

Placing her hand gently upon his head she said tenderly : "My child, remember the Belchnicell; mother loves you and wants you to be a good and happy boy?

Franz was naturally affectionate and loved the mother. Throwing both his arms round her neck he promised again. He really intended to be good for the moment, but more than all the children, by careless thoughtlessness, Franz had made the dear mother's heart ache.

All the morning the mother was busy getting the grand Christmas dinner, and here another great surprise awaited her. When she came to prepare the turkey, which the father had told her was a very heavy one, she found it stuffed with bright yellow goldens.

She gave the money to Hans, and when he told her there was enough for him to start a little business for himself, she felt that brighter days had indeed dawned upon them.

Very happy were they all after the visit of the good Kriss Kringle. Hans bought into a prosperous business that enabled the frugal Margarette to provide for her family, and promised in the future to prove a source of wealth to them.

The children, except baby Margarette, were sent to school, and were progressing finely, and the mother's tears and looks of care gave place to smiles and rosy cheeks.

On Saturday afternoon the father often managed to spare time to go to the pond with the boys. He loved to see them enjoy their holidays, and they were so fond of skating.

There were no boys in the village who could skate better than they, and the father was proud of their skill; but both he and the mother had forbidden them to venture upon the pond unless he was with them.

One beautiful moonlight night in March the father said : " There is to be a great concert at the Hall to-night, and you shall go and hear it, good wife. It is a pity, when we are doing so well, if you cannot have a treat now and then."

The mother smiled with pleasure. She had a sweet voice herself, and loved music dearly, but in her poverty she had not been able to indulge her taste, so of all things she thought she should enjoy the concert.

She put the children to bed, and after they had said their prayers she kissed them and bade them good night.

The father arranged the fire and made all safe, while the mother tied on her new bonnet and looked so pleased that the father kissed her, and said : "My dear wife is prettier now than any of the young girls."

Then they both laughed and went away very happy, and all the way to the Hall they talked hopefully of the future.

No sooner had they left the house than Franz got out of bed, and went to the window.

The clear full moon looked down upon the pond, covered with merry skaters, and their joyous shouts rang out upon the still night air, full of mirth and gladness. Franz stood for some time looking out at the window. At last he called to Karl, who was just going to sleep.

"Brother Karl!" he said, "all the boys and girls are out skating to-night, and it is getting so late that we cannot have much more fun this year. How I wish we could go too."

" Never mind!" said Karl, " come to bed now; if it freezes, father will go with us on Saturday."

" But," said Franz, " we might as well enjoy it as the rest of the boys; and I think it is mean of the father to make us stay in and go to bed. Come, Karl, get up and let us go out just a little while, the father will never know it."

" No, Franz," said Karl, " the mother never went to a concert before that I can remember, and I will not be the boy to disobey her while she is gone. I would rather do it when she is at home, if I am going to do it at all; and you ought not to call the good father mean ! "

But all Karl could say made no. difference. Franz was determined to go. " What a fool you are," said he, " you are never ready to have a good time;" and he took his skates and left Karl to go to sleep alone.

It was a lovely night, and though Franz knew he was doing very wrong, he ran down to the pond, and joining the skaters, soon was as merry as any of them.

"Now for a race," cried one of the boys, and off they started with a loud hurrah from the crowd.

"Do not go too far, boys," called an old fellow after them. "The ice is not over thick in the middle of the pond."

But the boys did not heed him.

On they went, Franz taking the lead, till from the shore they looked dim and shadowy in the silver white moonlight.

"Come, Franz, let us go back," said one of the larger boys. "The ice is getting thin."

"No," cried the excited boy; "I will cross the pond. Come on, boys! Come on!"

Away he sped quickly over the smooth

surface of the pond. He did not notice the others had turned back ; and he was a long way from them when he saw that he was alone, for they had skated as swiftly towards the shore as he from it.

"Perhaps I had better have staid with Karl. I suppose he is asleep now," thought Franz. "Oh, dear, I hope the mother will not find it out. I would rather the father would whip me than to see her look so sad ; but I will go home now."

Just as he turned around he saw something coming very swiftly toward him from the opposite shore. It seemed like a huge monster all covered with thick shaggy hair.

"What can it be?" thought Franz, very much frightened ; and he shouted as loud as possible to his companions ; but no one answered ; they were too far away to hear him. He cast a hurried glance behind. Nearer and nearer it came, the huge horrid shape, and well he knew in his heart it was the vengeful Belchnicell.

He tried to hasten, but his limbs trembled so much that he had little command over them. He dared not stop for a moment to take breath, though he was getting very tired. The Belchnicell drew nearer and nearer, till it seemed as though he could hear his heavy breathing.

A moment more and he would feel the horrid hot breath upon his cheek.

"I shall never see the mother again," thought the boy, in agony, "and the little Margarette. If I could only be in bed with Karl;" and the tears ran down his cheeks.

He exerted all his strength and pressed on. "If I could only reach the other boys before the horrid Belchnicell overtakes me, they could tell the mother."

Just then there was a loud, sharp sound, like the report of a pistol. It was the cracking of the ice, and in a moment it parted under Franz's feet, and he sank down, down into the cold waters of the pond.

How he was rescued from a watery grave no one can tell. The villagers found him floating on a large cake of ice, but his skates were gone forever.

They thought him dead when they carried him home, but while the father and mother rubbed him and wept over him, the good God gave him back to life. "Dear mother," whispered he, in a faint voice, as soon as he could speak, "I am so sorry I disobeyed you. Forgive me, mother."

Then the mother kissed him, and said: "Pray that the blessed Christ may forgive you as I do, my son."

Then Franz fell asleep, and all night the father and mother sat by his bedside watching.

He was sick for a long time with a burning fever, and when at last he recovered you would not have known him, he was so pale and thin; but he became a good, obedient boy, and no one of all the children was so tender and thoughtful for the dear mother as Franz.

Years passed away and the children grew up, married, and had little ones of their own; and always on Christmas day, the white-haired grandmother gathered them round her knee, and with their fair, rosy faces upraised to hers, they listened to the story of the Kriss Kringel and the Belchnicell.